AUTHOR......L

321.30944 KN

TITLE.........

D1076372

18

LA1

12.24.84

12-03-

04.89.

10.

09. 11. 85

09. 11. 85

08. 03. 86

LONDON BOROUGH OF
Wandsworth

05

BATTERSEA DISTRICT LIBRARY
LAVENDER HILL SW11 1JD
01- 228 3474 or 04- 228 8899

871 7466

THIS BOOK SHOULD BE RETURNED ON OR BEFORE THE
LATEST DATE SHOWN ON THIS LABEL OR THE CARD
INSERTED IN THE POCKET.

200 143 040 BD

KNIGHTS AND SAMURAI

Feudalism in Northern France and Japan

In the same series

VENICE AND AMSTERDAM
A study of seventeenth-century élites
by Peter Burke

Knights and Samurai

Feudalism in Northern France and Japan

ARCHIBALD LEWIS

TEMPLE SMITH · LONDON

First published in Great Britain 1974
by Maurice Temple Smith Ltd
37 Great Russell Street, London WC1
© 1974 Archibald R. Lewis
ISBN 0 8511 7043 9
Printed in Great Britain by
Lowe & Brydone (Printers) Ltd, Thetford, Norfolk

200143040

321.30944 LEW
D650848

CONTENTS

ILLUSTRATIONS

between pages 80 and 81

Tapestry from Northern France, c. AD 1500
Helmeted Merovingian warrior, c. AD 600
Helmeted Japanese guardian god from Nara, c. AD 742
Mounted Carolingian warriors, late 9th century
Mounted Japanese warriors, mid 13th century
Castle of Crac-des-Chevaliers, 12th and 13th centuries
Nagoya Castle of Ieyasu's time, early 17th century
Scene from a Kabuki play, late 17th century

MAPS

TO MY PARENTS
who loved Japan and her people

INTRODUCTION

For several generations historians who deal with Western Europe or those writing about Japan have made use of the term 'feudalism' to describe that system of aristocratic military and governmental control which for many centuries has seemed to represent the dominant force in each of these parts of the world. Indeed, the medieval knight and the Japanese *samurai* have, respectively, captured the popular imagination of both Western and Japanese civilizations and have filled song and story with their stirring and bloody deeds. Despite considerable scholarly research, however, it still remains unclear whether the feudal systems which produced these warriors truly resemble each other, although they obviously have a large measure of superficial similarity.

Furthermore, today we are much less sure than we were a decade ago that we fully understand the nature and development of Western European feudalism in general or Northern French feudalism in particular. This is because recent detailed research, which has concerned itself with various areas of France and periods of French history where feudalism flourished during the medieval era, has changed our views as to the kind of generalizations which can be made concerning it. And although our understanding of aspects of feudalism in medieval Japan seems clearer than that concerning medieval Europe, something of the same sort can be said about that, too. In the light of this uncertainty, it may serve a useful purpose to make an attempt, as this study does, to compare Northern French feudalism during its heyday with that of Japan up to the time of the Meiji Restoration. Such a study may help to explain aspects of the feudal development of each area which now seem puzzling, and may also assist us in forming an opinion as to whether or not they really are similar political and social systems.

Any such effort inevitably involves the scholar who has the temerity to attempt it in a need to assimilate and summarize an extensive body of scholarly research which he cannot hope to master thoroughly, especially since no one can ever be completely at home at the same time in the materials which bear upon Japanese and French feudal history. The author of this study must thus confess his profound dependence upon the work of other scholars. For instance, knowledgeable East

Asian specialists will recognize how much he has relied upon two recent syntheses of Japanese feudal history, John W. Hall's magnificent *Government and Local Power in Japan 500-1700* and Peter Duus's *Feudalism in Japan.* And while no comparable synthesis exists for Northern French feudalism, Western scholars will note how much he owes to the work of Bloch, Duby, Fawtier, Ganshof, Lemarignier, Strayer and Wood, to mention only a few of the talented historians whose insights have helped him understand Northern French developments.

There is also a select bibliography appended to this volume which, although incomplete, is added to help guide the interested reader to a fuller understanding of this difficult subject. It is limited to works written in French and English, but those who know Japanese should be aware of the fact that Professor Hall's work, mentioned above, has a particularly useful bibliography which lists recent important Japanese works dealing with Japan's feudal institutions. Similarly, the recent book by Professor Boutruche, *Seigneurie et féodalité II* contains many more references to Northern France than are found here.

The author also wishes to thank the University of Massachusetts, the University of Texas, the Fulbright Commission, the Ford Foundation and the American Council of Learned Societies for grants and leaves of absence which, over the years, have given him the opportunity to study the medieval societies of France and Japan, here and abroad, and to visit the areas he is treating in this volume. He is also indebted to Professor John W. Hall's Seminar in Japanese Feudal History at Yale University, which he visited in the spring of 1972, and which helped orientate him, and to Professor Richard Minear of the University of Massachusetts, who read the manuscript and made valuable suggestions concerning the Japanese portion of the text and illustrations. All errors are the author's own, but without such help they would be much more extensive.

Amherst, Massachusetts

CHAPTER I

The Northern French and Japanese Scenes

Northern France

The Northern France which formed the heartland where Western European feudalism developed and flourished between the time of the late Roman Empire and French Revolution was a part of Western Europe which had a certain unity of its own throughout most of this period.

In the first place, it possessed a certain overall geographical unity. It formed the westerly portion of that great Northern European plain of rolling forested lowlands and fertile river valleys which stretched from the Atlantic Ocean to Central Europe. It lay north of the mountainous Massif Central and east of a general Scheldt – Upper Moselle – Upper Rhône line and included within its boundaries the Seine and Loire river valleys. Since it faced the Atlantic, the English Channel and the North Sea, its climate was an Atlantic maritime one with heavy summer and winter rainfall, in contrast to lands to the south and east which tended to be more Mediterranean or continental in character. During the period which we are considering, this climate and soil made possible relatively abundant crops of wheat and rye over most of this area and a husbandry stressing livestock and fruit trees, as well as much exploitation of forest resources, while restricting dependable and profitable viniculture to areas which did not extend north of the Loire valley or Champagne.

To this geographical unity one should add an overall linguistic similarity in the speech of Northern France's inhabitants. Most of them, with the exception of some of those who lived in Brittany and Flanders and who spoke Celtic and Germanic dialects respectively, shared a common tongue which was to become modern French. This language was based upon the late vulgar Latin of Northern Gaul, with a few Germanic elements added to it, and had a number of regional variants. Nevertheless, it was a language quite different from the Provençal or Occitan which came to be spoken by the inhabitants of the Midi, so much so that during the high Middle Ages Northern France was known as the *Langue d'Oeil* to distinguish it from Southern France, which was called the *Langue d'Oc*.

In the third place, Northern France was a region which for centuries had had a certain historical unity. This began when it was a late Roman province and continued when much of the province formed the short-lived sub-Roman kingdom of Sygarius. After Clovis's conquest it mainly became the Neustria of Merovingian and early Carolingian times. When Louis the Pious divided his empire among his heirs, it formed that portion of the Kingdom of Francia which Charles the Bald ruled with little interference from his family rivals to the south and east. By the late ninth century its heartland formed a great marquisate of Neustria controlled by the Robertian house. And after this family had replaced the Carolingians as kings in 987, this same Northern France, as far south as the Limousin, the Massif Central, and the Lyonnais, represented that portion of the Capetian realm which really acknowledged this house as its monarchs, a situation which continued down to the end of the twelfth century.

Despite a measure of geographical, linguistic, and historial unity, however, Northern France was never isolated from the rest of Western Europe. Its rivers, which emptied into the Atlantic, the English Channel, and the North Sea, especially the last two, drew the Northern French to the salt water, from which it was only a short crossing to Britain, as Julius Caesar and William the Conqueror both demonstrated. In the same way the Meuse and Moselle made travel northeast into Belgium and the Rhinelands easy, just as was the case with the Rhône River and the plain of Aquitaine which led to the Mediterranean and the Iberian Peninsula. Along none of these routes were there any barriers between the Northern French and their immediate overseas or continental neighbours.

Similarly, it is worth noting that the linguistic differences which separated the inhabitants of Northern France from those of the Midi were not serious ones either, since both areas spoke tongues which were Romance in character, while to the east many of those who lived in Lorraine, Eastern Burgundy, and Western Switzerland spoke Northern French dialects. And, thanks to the Norman Conquest, throughout most of this period the upper classes of Britain used a French which was at least understandable in the Île-de-France and which as late as the eighteenth century had survived as the Law French of British Courts. And if French was well known to the upper classes of the British Isles, it was also spoken by a larger group of aristocrats and others who dominated the Kingdom of Two Sicilies, Cyprus, Syria, and Palestine and Frankish Greece during many centuries. The native tongue of Northern France, then, was not so much a barrier to wider communication as an upper-class international lingua franca hardly less important than medieval Latin or Provençal.

We must also remember that Northern France, despite local peculiarities, shared a common religious faith and church organization with the rest of Western Europe. It acknowledged the authority of a distant Papacy, mirrored a general Western European secular church organization, and shared a regard for a special type of monasticism common to its neighbours. It remained a part of Western Christendom during these centuries, with all that that implied.

Finally, one must note that Northern France, despite its historical distinctiveness, was always part of a larger political structure. First, it was a province of the later Roman Empire, then a part of the much larger *Regnum Francorum* or Frankish Empire of the Merovingians and Carolingians, and finally, the heartland of a larger Kingdom of Francia which in theory included areas which lay south of the Cevennes. For more than a century a large part of it also comprised a portion of a Norman-Angevin Empire which included most of Britain, while many of its leading aristocratic families acquired crowns and lordships which stretched throughout the Mediterranean all the way from the Jordan and the Bosphorus to the borders of Moorish Spain. Politically, as well as geographically, linguistically, and religiously, Northern France was part of a much wider international world.

Japan

Japan's distinctiveness during the period when her feudal institutions were developing and flourishing was, of course, much more marked than that enjoyed by Northern France, as one might expect after glancing at a map.

In the first place she had and still has a distinct geographical unity, based upon the fact that her civilization was centred on four main islands, Hokkaido, Honshū, Shikoku, and Kyūshū, which lie off the shores of Korea and Northern China in the waters of East Asia's Northern Pacific Ocean. In studying feudal Japan, however, one should exclude from calculation Hokkaido and Northern Honshū and centre attention upon that area stretching from the plain of the Kantō (close to Modern Tōkyō) south to Kyūshū. Here lay the heartland of medieval and early modern Japan, around its ancient capitals of Nara and Kyōto in the mountains near the headwaters of the Inland Sea.

In the second place one needs to note that Japan's geographical

unity was reinforced by the fact that her main islands were mountainous and heavily forested with only limited amounts of fertile soil
fit for agriculture along coastal plains and in narrow river valleys. Here
a combination of heavy monsoon rains and carefully constructed irriga-
tion systems had early made possible an intensive cultivation of rice in
small paddies, except in Northern Honshū and Hokkaido, thus providing the Japanese with the grain that formed their staple diet. At the
same time these rains also made possible a luxurious forest growth
of bamboo, pine, and deciduous trees which gave the land a forest
character quite different from that which prevailed in much of East
Asia's mainland. In contrast to the stock raising, wheat cultivation
and fruit production which moulded the agriculture of Northern
France, Japan always relied upon an intensive rice culture combined
with the use of her northern monsoon forest to form her basic economy.
And despite the fact that quite early Japanese clansmen possessed
horses which they prized and which were perhaps inherited from the
Central Asian past of some of Japan's inhabitants, her civilization
had no real livestock element in its agriculture. Instead it relied upon
the spade and the hard labour of its rice-growing peasants for the
sustained yields which fed the population.

To this special geographical and climatic element which helped
make Japan unique, one needs to add a distinct linguistic unity, too.
Although the Japanese are a very mixed people racially speaking, by
historic times they seemed to have developed a language of their own
quite different from that spoken in nearby Korea and mainland China
and only found in somewhat different form along the Ryukyu Island
chain that stretches south towards Formosa. This unique tongue still
distinguishes the Japanese from their East Asian neighbours.

Thirdly, Japan kept from earlier times some rather unusual primitive
religious elements in her civilization which are still preserved in her
great Shinto shrines such as Ise and which are revealed in the peculiar
way she has always regarded her Imperial line and her family system.
This set of religious ideas has tended to cause the Japanese to modify
outside religious ideas which have reached them from other areas of
the Asian continent into forms and institutions adapted to their own
special civilization.

Finally, related to the above factors, throughout the entire period
which we are considering the Japanese always had a centralized government and a common set of political institutions, except in those
frontier areas to the north which were inhabited by every different
tribal Ainu peoples who were slowly and inexorably being conquered

and absorbed by a Japanese advance. This centralized political structure was to prove powerful enough to resist a Mongol attempt to conquer Japan in the thirteenth century and during the sixteenth to overcome local centres of authority to form the united Japan of early modern times.

However clear it is that Japan's geographical, linguistic, religious, and political distinctiveness was always more marked than that of Northern France during the period we are discussing, it would be wise not to overemphasize that fact. For instance, communication by sea across the narrow Tsushima Straits to Korea was never difficult, nor was it hard to follow the islands south to China and the Pescadores. Hence, foreign influences were constantly modifying Japanese insularity and at quite an early date had made her part of East Asian civilization, as can be clearly seen when one examines her religious ideas, her political institutions, or her culture. For instance, if Japan's spoken togue was unique, quite early she began to use Chinese characters in her written language, so that most Japanese words other than verb forms have always been intelligible to one who knows written Chinese.

In addition to all this, during certain periods of her history, and especially throughout the seventh, eighth, and ninth centuries, Japan's rulers deliberately copied the Chinese system of imperial government, law and administration and acknowledged the theoretical supremacy of the T'ang Sons of Heaven. Later on, when the Japanese, during the eleventh, twelfth, and thirteenth centuries, developed their military shōgunate, it is worth noting that nearby Korea evolved a military and governmental system that was not too dissimilar. And who has not been struck by the way in which Tokugawa Shōguns welcomed the Confucian ideas and ideals which were current in the Ming and Ch'ing China of their day?

Nor were the Japanese ever immune to outside religious concepts. Regularly, and especially during the Nara period, Buddhism and Confucian ideas flowed into Japan from the Chinese mainland and even from more remote parts of the Asian continent. So, too, did art forms and technological processes of great importance, until Japan was clearly a part of a wider civilized world.

Thus Japan's inhabitants throughout the centuries covered by this study, despite their distinctive geography, climate, and religious and political systems, were never completely isolated from their East Asian neighbours. Rather their culture came to bear the imprint of this outside world and was always closer to that of China and Korea than some scholars have been willing to acknowledge.

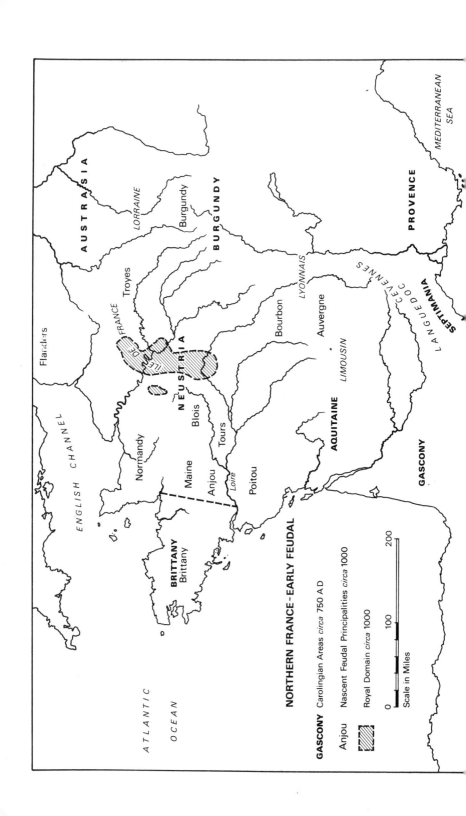

NORTHERN FRANCE - EARLY FEUDAL

GASCONY   Carolingian Areas *circa* 750 A.D.

Anjou   Nascent Feudal Principalities *circa* 1000

Royal Domain *circa* 1000

Scale in Miles

0   100   200

MEDITERRANEAN
SEA

AUSTRASIA

LORRAINE

Burgundy

BURGUNDY

Troyes

LYONNAIS

PROVENCE

FRANCE

ÎLE DE

NEUSTRIA

Bourbon

Auvergne

CÉVENNES

LANGUEDOC

SEPTIMANIA

Flanders

ENGLISH CHANNEL

Normandy

Blois

Tours

Maine

Anjou

Loire

Poitou

LIMOUSIN

AQUITAINE

GASCONY

BRITTANY
Brittany

ATLANTIC

OCEAN

CHAPTER II

Feudal Beginnings

Northern France, A.D. 400-687

During the last century of the Roman Empire the Northern France where Western European feudalism had its origins was a land of great villa estates owned by a privileged senatorial aristocracy, who cultivated them using the labour of a peasantry, tied to the soil as state serfs or *coloni* by Imperial edict. These peasants not only grew crops upon such estates for the aristocracy, but were also required to pay heavy dues and taxes to support the Empire's armies and its swollen bureaucracy.

By 476 the collapse of the Western Empire marked the end of most of its machinery of government and its armies, but not of the villa system of Northern Gaul, except in certain restricted regions such as Brittany and Flanders. Elsewhere, once Frankish rule had been established by Clovis and his immediate successors, and the Franks had found homes for themselves upon lands which were largely taken over from the Imperial *fisc*, within a century a certain mingling and amalgamation of upper-class Franks and Romans took place, just as it did in the lower levels of society, too. A new powerful barbarized rural aristocracy held sway over Northern French areas, most of whose peasants found themselves little freer than they had been during the last years of the Empire.

Despite the efforts of Merovingian rulers to maintain the Roman system of administration, it steadily decayed. Merovingian peripatetic courts did not resemble late Roman Imperial capitals such as Trier and Milan, nor was their central administration anything but a rather sad echo of that found in Ravenna or Constantinople. As the decades wore on taxation simply ceased, and law courts, increasingly barbarized, enforced procedures like those found in Salic Law Codes which were quite different from those prescribed by Roman Law. In place of Roman provincial officialdom a simpler system of Frankish counts and dukes came to prevail, making use of men who combined in their person the military, civil and judicial authority of the king, which they exercised as viceroys on the local level. Or we find much power in the hands of bishops, who tended to rule over the older decayed *civitates.* By the seventh century it was a sub-Roman, semi-barbarous civilization which prevailed in Northern France under Merovingian rule.

It was during these decades when the Roman Empire was collapsing and the simpler, cruder administration of the Merovingians was taking over that we find appearing the first elements of what was to become the feudalism of a later age. These were the result of forces, practices, and forms which were derived from the both the late Roman and the Germanic worlds and which had begun to be combined and fused in a special way.

The first aspect of this new feudal tendency was the emergence of the private armed retainer. Such warriors had a double origin, partly Roman, partly German. During the troubled last century of the Western Roman Empire important landowners or magnates began to protect their estates and privileges by assembling private bands of armed retainers known as *bucellarii.* Late Roman Law codes forbade such followers, but there is evidence that they were particularly numerous in Gaul. Meanwhile, Germans who entered the Empire, first as mercenary soldiers and then as victors, brought with them a somewhat similar system which as early as the second century A.D. had existed across the Rhine, according to Tacitus. This system was one whereby freeborn German warriors would attach themselves to a war-chief and form his private warband, swearing loyalty to him until death in return for provender in his household and a share of war booty. Since the best troops in the late Roman Imperial army were generally Germans, both generals and Emperors relied upon this *comitatus* system to recruit bodyguards, like the Franks who served Constantine in this capacity and whom he very much prized.

It is not surprising then that, after the Empire had disappeared in Northern France and the Franks had taken over, their kings continued such practices and recruited bodyguards of special warriors known as *antrustiones* who were bound to these monarchs by the same ties of loyalty as those held by the members of the Germanic *comitatus.* These *antrustiones*, who also resembled late Roman *bucellarii*, were often of slave origin, had a triple *wergeld* or blood money payment if they were killed or injured, and were sometimes rewarded for their loyal service by being given high official posts, even the charge of counts who ruled the provinces of the *Regnum Francorum.*

It was not only Frankish kings, however, who began to recruit such armed retainers; so, too, did the leading magnates of Merovingian Gaul who are called *procures* in the documents. They tended to assemble bands of private retainers to protect their interests, and these came to be called *vassi* or *vassali*, terms derived from the Celtic word *gwass* meaning servant. Such retainers were frequently of servile origin during the sixth century, but in the course of the seventh they began to rise in the social scale and were often drawn from other elements in society. The use of a Celtic word for such followers, incidentally, is interesting and suggests that when the Roman Empire collapsed, elements of a submerged pre-Roman Gallic social system were reappearing.

Furthermore, it seems probable that the number and the importance of these retainers was due to certain technological changes which began to affect the practices of warfare. These changes seem to have appeared first of all in Italy where, during the course of the sixth century, warfare increasingly came to depend upon a use of heavily armed cavalry, using stirrups and armed with lances, who rode to battle upon great warhorses. It was with such *cataphracti*, as they were called, who were largely recruited from among barbarian peoples, that Justinian's generals, Belisarius and Narses, captured Italy from the Ostrogoths. Maurice, the last great Byzantine Emperor of the sixth century, according to the *Pseudo-Strategicon*, used them, too, in defending his Italian domains against the Lombards. By the seventh century, if not earlier, the Franks, who invaded Italy repeatedly, had begun to use more such horsemen in their campaigns, although the freeborn foot-soldier, who owed military service to the king and was mustered for battle by the count, remained the mainstay of Frankish military might. At any rate, whenever and wherever they appeared, these horsemen required special expensive warhorses and equipment and training which ordinary levies could not be expected to possess, but which *vassi* could. Hence an increase in the number of such retainers who could be armed in this fashion was the direct result of a need for their use in battle.

Warbands, especially if they were well-trained mounted ones, could be maintained by kings or magnates as part of their households. But it often proved easier to reward them for their service by allotting them estates which they could rely on to maintain themselves between campaigns. Such land, given to a warrior in return for personal military service, was sometimes known as a *precarium*, or, since minimum payments were made for it by a retainer, as a *beneficium*. In either case the magnate kept the ownership of this property and gave his follower the

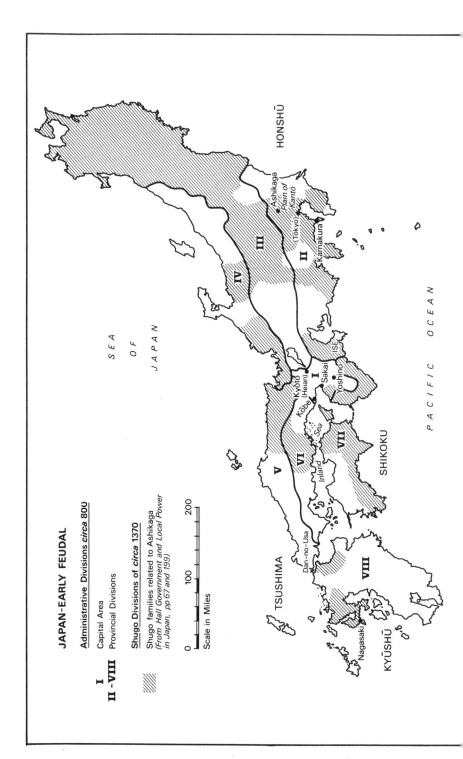

JAPAN-EARLY FEUDAL

Administrative Divisions *circa* 800

I Capital Area
II - VIII Provincial Divisions

Shugo Divisions of *circa* 1370

Shugo families related to Ashikaga
*(From Hall Government and Local Power
in Japan, pp 67 and 199)*

Scale in Miles

0 100 200

SEA

OF

JAPAN

HONSHŪ

Ashikaga
Plain of
Kantō

(Tōkyō)

Kamakura

Kyōto (Heian)

Kōbe

Sakai

Yoshino

ISE

Inland
Sea

PACIFIC OCEAN

SHIKOKU

Dan-no-Usa

TSUSHIMA

Nagasaki

KYŪSHŪ

I II III IV V VI VII VIII

use or usufruct of it, generally for a lifetime. Nor were such *precaria* or *beneficia* only created by landowners to pay for private military service. They could also arise in another way when small landowners, who were insecure and unable to protect themselves, gave their land to a powerful magnate and received it back as a *precarium*. Either way what arose was a system of landholding by dependants on a lifetime usufruct basis which was often founded upon military service.

Such arrangements had become so common and so regularized in Frankish Gaul by the seventh century that they resulted in the appearance of a special type of private contract between magnate and retainer, known as *commendation*, whose form has been preserved for us in regular *formularies*. They show us that a *commendation* was a contract specifying the exact terms of service owed a magnate by his retainer and vice versa, and that such such retainers were now increasingly known as *vassi* or *vassali*. And we find that increasingly the payment given to a retainer by a magnate in return for his service is stated to be the lifetime use of a piece of land.

Finally we should also note that quite a few estates, especially those controlled by great ecclesiastical landowners, the bishops and abbots, began to be exempted from both royal taxation and the encroachment of royal officials through the grant of special charters of immunity by the kings of the period. As this trend continued, it meant that a growing number of lay and church landowners escaped all control by the central government and became almost supreme in their own domains.

It must not be supposed, however, that anything like a feudal system, that is to say a network of personal relationship that took the place of government, was yet established in seventh-century Northern France. Though government was rudimentary in character, it was still based on the supreme power of the Merovingian ruler, who delegated authority to the counts and dukes who served as his all-but-independent viceroys in the provinces. These latter kept their public character and continued to muster the local militia, levy royal dues, and preside over local regional courts in a way which was relatively effective. What was new was a growing network of personal relationships which allowed great landowners to recruit armed followed by private agreement and pay them with grants of land from estates which increasingly possessed an immunity from taxation or interference from public officials. Then, after Dagobert's death in 639, Merovingian monarchs steadily lost control over outlying parts of their *Regnum Francorum* to such magnates, who were not only supreme in their estates, but also began to take over the offic℩ of duke or count as well in the provinces in which they lived.

As this happened, still another development took place which decreased the authority of the Merovingian kings who ruled Northern France. This was the appearance of a special official at their courts known as the *Major Domo* or *Mayor of the Palace.* Increasingly this official came to exercise hereditary authority in the name of the king and to exclude the latter from power, until by the late seventh century the heirs of Clovis had become shadowy long-haired princes dominated by their Mayors of the Palace and exercising little authority over either their court or their outlying territories. Such was the situation on the eve of a great change which modified both the Merovingian world of Northern France and the future of feudalism—the rise to supreme power of a new Carolingian family.

Heian Japan, A.D. 794-1185

In the year 794 Japan's Imperial capital was moved from Nara to nearby Kyōto (then called Heian), which ushered in a new period in its medieval history. Yet the Imperial centuries at Nara were to prove as important for Japan's development as those of the Roman Empire and the Merovingians were in laying the basic for much of the later society of Northern France. Here, during the course of the seventh and eighth centuries, the institutions of a tribal Japan, only recently united by its Yamato Emperors, were transformed into a new system which was to affect all subsequent Japanese history. What appeared at Nara was a new civil monarchy, based on Buddhist and Confucian principles which had come from China and which were grafted on to an Imperial house claiming descent from the Sun Goddess and reflected and embodied in a special series of law codes, completed by 718, having been copied from those of T'ang China.

This new civil monarchy was centred in and based upon a newly created Imperial city which housed not only the Emperor but also a centralized Imperial bureaucracy. To support Emperor, capital, and administration, a new taxation and land distribution system was gradually established throughout civilized Japan. Under this arrangement all peasants became state serfs living on rice lands and other cultivated fields which were the theoretical property of the Emperor, though such humble cultivators were allowed the use of fertile land which, in theory at least, was to be redivided among peasant families every six years on the basis of peasant family size. In return for this, peasants were expected to serve in the army, when summoned to do so, to pay a portion of the rice and other crops they raised as taxes, and to perform special labour services as well. Crops paid as taxes were either carried by the peasants to the capital to support the Emperor and his court and bureaucracy or taken to provincial centres to support officials who were located there.

In this new monarchy all officials of the central government, first at Nara and then at Kyōto, were appointed by the Emperor, as were some three score provincial governors. On the other hand, on the more local level, it was the provincial governors who appointed those local chiefs who were in direct charge of the peasant population. And though in theory the central administration was chosen, as in China, by examination, in practice it seems clear that during the Nara period local clan aristocrats tended to be brought into the system and to become the local officials and the court aristocracy who made the government function. Finally, in place of the tribal warriors of an earlier Japan, a new army was created. This was recruited from the ranks of the peasantry who owed the Emperor military service and was organized into guard units, some of whom were stationed in the capital, while others served in provincial centres. A few special garrisons were stationed along frontiers in Northern Japan where the Japanese still faced unconquered Ainu tribesmen.

Such was the system established at Nara and transferred to the new capital of Kyōto in 794. Once in Kyōto, however, this governmental and social system gradually began to change and to be modified in a number of ways. The first change was a steady decrease in the authority which was directly exercised by the Emperors themselves. In part this may have been the result of the fact that many Heian Emperors either died young or succeeded to their authority as boys, as was the case with the later Merovingians. But whatever the cause, we soon find Imperial power usurped by a great court family known as the Fujiwaras. The Fujiwaras, like Merovingian Mayors of the Palace, seized power by dominating certain high offices, such as that of regent and chancellor, and by marrying their daughters increasingly to reigning Emperors. As a result of all this, by the tenth century it was they who ruled, while the Yamato Emperors only reigned. ✗

A second change which took place during this period was a growing cleavage between the cultivated court aristocrats and dignitaries and their provincial counterparts who ran the provinces. The 'World of the Shining Prince', where effete, cultivated court officials flourished, became increasingly remote from the mundane life of the provinces. Cultivated aristocrats of the court had little in common with their rural counterparts, and the latter became alienated from Kyōto and its officials.

Finally as Emperors became figureheads and court aristocrats increasingly effete and do-nothing, the landholding system of the Nara era began to break down. This was caused by the rise of private estates in the countryside. Such estates, known as *shōen*, were rice lands and other fields which were given special rights of immunity so that they no longer paid taxes or dues levied upon public lands in general. It is significant that during this period there was a growing tendency, under the *Insei* system, for Emperors and ex-Emperors, court officials, and local aristocrats to accumulate this kind of property, and as this took place the entire system of government based upon public lands began to decay. *Shōen*, made up of scattered plots or paddies of rice lands and other territory under private control, grew in number, especially on land which was newly cleared and put into cultivation, and with them a growing immunity of such land from public duties and taxation, as was the case in Merovingian Gaul.

As this happened, it is interesting to note that Heian Japan developed its own counterpart to the Frankish *precarium*, which was known as the *shiki,* and which represented a right to a fixed proportion of rice and other crops produced upon a *shōen* estate, whether this *shiki* belonged to an estate owner, an estate steward, an outside 'protector', or the peasant cultivator himself. By the tenth century a new system of owning, controlling, and dividing the proceeds from the rich agricultural lands of Japan had appeared, and this helped destroy the governmental and social system which had appeared at Nara some centuries earlier.

What is equally important in Heian Japan during these years is the gradual growth in the provinces of new bands of private warriors. These seem to have arisen as the military system of Nara decayed, its place being taken by local warriors who were also landlords. As one would expect, such warrior bands were especially numerous in regions like the Kantō plain of North Central Honshū which were far from Kyōto and close to the still-expanding internal frontiers of Japan. When we first see these warriors, they appear to be heavily armed horsemen, using the bow and the sword, who ride into battle and tend to dominate the peasantry and the local government of their districts by almost hereditary right.

Their organization was an interesting one. Each band seems to have been controlled by a family chief and was composed of members of his own or his extended family and its dependents. Members of this warband who were related to its chief were called 'sons of the house'. Others, not related, who also served as warriors, were known as housemen or *kenin*, and still lowlier dependents as *rōtō*. Such men, who seem quite similar to the *vassi* and *vassali* of Merovingian Gaul, served their lord until death, though we find evidence of no special ceremony which formalized such a relationship, like the *commendation* used in Northern France.

These family warbands grew in importance in the provinces, and as early as 935 they were powerful enough to defy with success local authorities who were appointed by the central government. After 1000 they began to take over whole provinces and to organize themselves into family confederacies which dominated regional areas. When they did so, the leaders of such confederacies began to be known as warrior chieftains or *bushi no tōryō*.

Once firmly established in the countryside by the late eleventh and twelfth centuries, they began to extend their activities into the capital itself, where the court aristocrats, ex-Emperors, and the large monasteries found such warriors useful in protecting their interests. As this happened, two main rival families of warrior chieftains became important, both of which were descended from collateral branches of the Imperial house established by ninth-century Emperors. One of these was the Seiwa branch of the Minamoto clan; the other, the Ise branch of the Taira family. The Taira were particularly powerful in Western Japan, at Kyōto, and around the Inland Sea. The Minamoto tended to dominate the East and especially the Kantō plain.

As one would expect, a struggle developed between these two warrior alliances at court and elsewhere in Japan and lasted for almost a generation. At first the Taira were victorious. Finally, between 1180 and 1185, in a struggle known as the Gempei War, the Minamoto alliance of warbands led by a certain Yoritomo overcame their rivals and were victorious. By 1185 Japan lay at their feet, just as in 687 in Merovingian Gaul the Carolingian house had finally defeated its family rivals who served as Mayors of the Palace in Neustria. A new age had dawned for Japan.

Some similarities and differences

At first glance, one cannot help but be struck by the similarities in the way in which proto-feudal elements developed in Merovingian Northern France and Heian Japan. In both areas they appeared after an earlier Imperial and central authority had decayed. And in both in the end new leaders of warrior bands, who were tied together by a network of personal private relationships, took over the central authority.

It is also worth noting that in both Heian Japan and Merovingian domains this process was assisted by the profound changes in a previous system of landholding. In Northern France during Merovingian times these changes meant the end of the older Roman taxation system and state serfdom of the peasantry and new immunities acquired by the owners of large estates. In Heian Japan we find a decay of state control over the peasant rice lands and other agricultural village systems and the appearance of new private estates, called *shōen*, which also gained an immunity from the taxes and dues which had been levied by the central government. Each made use of conditional grants or the usufruct of some of these estates to dependents, *precaria* or benefices in Northern France, *shiki* in Japan. In both areas the period saw the appearance of a new class of heavily armed horsemen who became the élite fighting forces of the time, replacing an older reliance upon the militia foot-soldier.

On the other hand, there were also certain differences between the two areas. Merovingian government and society, which produced new proto-feudal elements, was from the start relatively weak in the institutions of its central governmental structure and in the local officials who were connected with its royal rule. And even these had lost much of their cohesion and authority by the seventh century. Heian Japan, however, long after 1185, kept both its capital and its official class in the provinces and bequeathed this governmental system to the next age in Japanese history. Even the warring alliances of the Taira and Minamoto clans had close family ties with the Imperial house itself, being cadet branches of the Yamato family, in contrast to the Carolingians who has fewer ties with the Merovingian line of kings.

Yet there was less of a military continuity between the older system and the new in Heian Japan than was true in Merovingian France. By the eleventh century the older traditions of military service seem to have completely disappeared in Japan, so that the Taira and Minamoto operated in a military vacuum where older military formations had ceased to function and which they hastened to fill. In seventh-century Northern France, however, the mounted warriors of a Pepin the Old were not alone in bearing arms, for so too did freeborn warriors who were mustered as foot-soldiers by the counts and dukes of the period, and who continued to serve in battle during the next age of Carolingian control.

Thus different continuities tend to distinguish each area. In Japan the continuity was governmental, court, and Imperial in nature. In Merovingian France it was local and military for the most part. And these differences were to continue during the years to come.

CHAPTER III

Formative Feudalism

The Carolingian era in Northern France, A.D. 687-900

In 687 Pepin of Heristal (680-714), the head of the Carolingian family and Mayor of the Palace of Austrasia, led his counts and his armed followers to a victory over the Mayor of the Palace of Neustria, and reunited the *Regnum Francorum.* During the next eight decades he and his able successors, Charles Martel (714-41) and Pepin the Short (741-68), gradually extended their authority over outlying parts of Merovingian domains until by 752 most of them were under their direct control, except for Frisia, Brittany, Bavaria, and Aquitaine which still kept a large measure of autonomy.

In the course of extending their authority, first in the name of do-nothing Merovingian monarchs and then on their own account, they faced one dangerous foe, the Moslems from Spain who had crossed the Pyrenees in 718, established themselves in Languedoc and Provence, and were raiding north into Aquitaine and Central France. In 732 Charles Martel checked these raiders in a battle fought near Poitiers. Then he and Pepin drove them south, conquering Provence and parts of Aquitaine in the process until by 752 the Moslems had been confined to a few cities in Septimania. By the time of Pepin's death in 768 these Moors had been pushed into Spain, Aquitainian particularism had been crushed, and a suzerainty had been established over the Gascons who lived on the Gallic side of the Pyrenees.

In reconquering these outlying provinces and in driving out the Moors, the early Carolingian rulers operated quite differently from their Merovingian predecessors. In the first place, they formed a close alliance with the Church, especially in Germany. Secondly, since their campaigns called for the use of large numbers of heavily armed cavalry-men who, because of the need for troops capable of waging war on distant fronts, were the élite troops of the period, they increased the number of their *vassi* who were linked to them by personal ties and rewarded them with large grants of land so that they could support themselves as mounted warriors. Some of this land consisted of estates given outright to these *vassi* from property belonging to the

Carolingian family or confiscated from its opponents. Much of the land given them, however, was in the form of *precaria* or benefices. And since demand for such estates exceeded supply, all the earlier Carolingians, and especially Pepin the Short, took over considerable Church property which they distributed to their loyal followers as *precaria*, although nominal Church ownership continued to be recognised. These Church *precaria*, known as *precaria verbo regis*, or *precaria* by order of the king, were especially numerous in Neustria, Burgundy, and western Austrasia, that is to say Northern France.

Thus, by the time of Pepin's death, there had come to be a great increase in vassalage and the use of *precaria* and benefices throughout Northern France, for such tenures were not only popular with Carolingian rulers, but with their great magnates, too, who copied their princes in increasing the number of their own mounted *vassi* retainers in the same way. As this happened, vassals, especially those owing loyalty and service to the Carolingians, tended to rise in the social scale. Vassalage now became an honourable relationship which involved most of the landed aristocracy and a coveted status for one eager to gain power and prestige.

One further change took place during this same period which was to affect formative Carolingian feudalism. In 754 Pepin the Short, called into Italy by the Pope to check Lombard attacks upon Rome, led an army across the Alps and defeated the Lombards. But even before this expedition he had received Papal backing in replacing the Merovingians as rulers with his own family and had been crowned King of the Franks by Pope Stephen in 752. Henceforth Carolingian monarchs were even more closely allied with the Church than had previously been the case. Indeed, in Francia and elsewhere they were now in control of it, with the Popes as distant junior partners. Rebellion against the Carolingians was rebellion against God's anointed. Carolingian authority had assumed a theocratic basis, and this was to lead directly to the Western Empire of Charlemagne and Louis the Pious and a Caesaro-papism which almost matched that of nearby Byzantine emperors.

Under Charlemagne (768-814) the work of his predecessors continued in a number of ways. Charlemagne expanded his state in all directions—south into Spain where he conquered a Spanish march and into Italy where in 774 he annexed the Lombard Kingdom and the Duchies of Rome and Ravenna, as well as east into Germany where Frisia, Saxony, Bavaria, and Slavic marches were incorporated into his Empire. In 800 he was crowned Western Roman Emperor by the Pope.

Such distant campaigning required large contingents of mounted warriors, so Charlemagne continued to grant estates to fighting men who served him as *vassi*, especially to an élite group known as *vassi dominici*, or vassals of my lord king. Some of the latter were maintained in his household, but in time most were given estates on a lifetime basis with which to support themselves, and they were then known as *vassi casati*, or vassals who had been sent forth. Some of these estates were carved out of land belonging to the royal *fisc*, especially in newly annexed regions near frontiers. A considerable number of them, however, came from property in Northern France which belonged to the Carolingian family. And Charlemagne encouraged his magnates to distribute similar benefices to their own *vassi* and thus to increase the size of the mounted forces they could bring with them to his campaigns. Though all freeborn men continued to owe the monarch military service when called out, and were regularly mustered for war on a local basis by Carolingian-appointed counts, a growing percentage of the effective armed forces was composed of such mounted royal vassals and those of the monarch's prominent noble followers.

Charlemagne found this kind of vassalage so effective that he began to make use of it in ways which were increasingly non-military in character. Thus he and his son Louis the Pious (814-40) and his grandson Charles the Bald (843-77) began to tie their officials, the counts and dukes, to their person by ties of vassalage, and the governmental charges given to these officials, known as *honors*, in some ways began to resemble benefices given to vassals in return for military service. Soon similar ties were established between these monarchs and their leading churchmen, the abbots, the bishops, and the archbishops, for Carolingian rulers were the effective heads of the Church within their Empire.

By the early ninth century all this also resulted in more formal ways in which such proto-feudal relationships came to be regularized in ceremonies where *commendation* and oaths of fidelity took place and where vassals placed themselves in a subordinate relationship to their monarchs. Such procedures were regulated by Carolingian *capitularies* of the period, and great lords were encouraged to follow royal practice in such matters. The upper ranks of Carolingian society found such arrangements so desirable that the tie of vassalage could be described as of supreme importance in the advice which that great noble lady Dhuoda gave in 843 to her son Count William, who was a leading magnate of Francia. The loyalty this system prescribed between a vassal and his royal lord, according to Dhuoda, was still amorphous as to duties and somewhat negative in nature but very important to all concerned none the less.

As the number of vassals increased during the rest of the ninth century in Northern France, other changes began to take place in this proto-feudal or pre-feudal system of vassalage. First of all there developed a certain union, almost legal in character, between vassalage as a tie of loyalty and the benefice or *honor* given to a vassal by his king or his lord. This took place despite the fact that vassals could still possess private allodial property of their own, which was not a benefice, and one could still be a landless vassal who was maintained in the household of one's lord.

Secondly, though ultimate legal ownership of a benefice still remained in the hands of the monarch or lord who granted it out to a vassal, he who received it *in fact* increasingly began to exercise the right of handing it on to his heirs. This hereditability of benefices, and of *honors* as well, became especially common in Northern France.

In the third place it became possible for a man to enter into a number of vassalage arrangements and to receive benefices from more than one lord, which, of course, strained the ties of loyalty which should have existed between a vassal and his royal overlord. In short, if one conceives of vassalage as an arrangement used by Carolingian monarchs to strengthen their authority over their officials, their churchmen and their fighting men, one can see that now it had became something quite different and had ceased to serve as a stabilizing force in the society of late ninth-century Northern France.

Furthermore, one more development began to take place late in this century, if not somewhat earlier. Many powerful noble landlords began to transform the benefices given to them by kings, churchmen, and other nobles into allodial property over which they could exercise exclusive rights of ownership and control in hereditary fashion, unconcerned about duties owed to kings or other magnates for them. They were often able to do so with the express consent of monarchs who were bidding for support from their nobility during the endemic civil wars which we find in Northern France after 829. Or they were able to do so illegally when Viking invasions made ordinary government increasingly difficult to maintain and strained royal authority to the limit. Either way, when such a transformation of benefices took place, it weakened proto-feudal relationships profoundly and set up in their place a system of hereditary allodial seigneuries whose lords were tied to little except their own immediate interests on a local level.

As great lords assumed allodial ownership of their land or made their benefices hereditary, this of course weakened royal power in Northern France profoundly. But so too did the constant civil wars which Carolingian heirs of Louis the Pious insisted upon waging against one another, and those which Carolingians and Robertians, as claimants to the throne, fought late in the century. Even more decisive in causing royal authority to lose its effectiveness were the Viking invasions of this same period, for Viking attacks, which affected most of Northern France for many decades, could not be checked by the cumbersome defence system which Carolingian military practices provided, despite the building of a number of new fortresses. Nor did the custom of paying them blackmail in the form of massive *danegelds* do more than whet their aggressive appetites. All that happened was that it became increasingly clear that Northern French rulers could not defend their realm and thus could not govern effectively. As an understanding of this fact grew, royal authority disintegrated everywhere. As a result, secular and ecclesiastical magnates transformed their hereditary monarchy into an elective affair at the very moment when they were tending to make their own estates and *honors* hereditary. By 900 Northern France still recognized the theoretical authority of its kings, but had in fact become a welter of competing secular and ecclesiastical lordships with varying vestiges of proto-feudal practices and arrangements attached to them, which were to affect the way they were to be governed during the harsh first feudal age to follow.

It may seem somewhat paradoxical to insist at this point that ninth-century proto-feudal developments and relationships and a final relapse into anarchical disorder by 900 were accompanied by certain more constructive developments. But this seems to be true, especially in the fields of agriculture and of trade and commerce, which laid the foundations of a sound future progress. Let us first examine agricultural changes during this period.

Between the last years of Charlemagne's reign and the death of Louis the Pious, we have evidence that the rural population Northern France began to increase and that this resulted in a movement to clear the forested waste in the Seine river valley and to begin to drain the swamps of maritime Flanders. Great proprietors encouraged this agricultural progress and lay and ecclesiastical landlords began to organize their estates more effectively, as we can see from records such as the *Polyptych of St Irminon* of the Abbey of Saint Germain-des-Prés near Paris or when we study Charlemagne's *Capitulary de villis* or details from other establishments in Champagne. This agrarian progress was unfortunately halted by the destruction which Viking raids brought to much of the Northern French countryside. But it did lay the basis for much later development in the years to come.

Equally interesting are signs of a quickening of internal and external commerce throughout the entire ninth century. Royal monetary policy had something to do with this. Charlemagne reformed the coinage and opened new mints, and his successors continued his policies. This helped to cause a growth of trading centres, or embryo towns, over much of the region and the development of a number of rural markets where exchange of goods took place. These trading centres began to attract groups of merchants who were active in commerce locally and on the wider international scene. Evidence from coin finds, for instance, dating from these years, shows that money had begun to circulate widely throughout most of Northern France.

It seems probable that Viking raids did not hinder these developments as much as they did agricultural progress, for what the Vikings took in one region they tended to trade in another. In short, if the late ninth century showed a decay of royal authority and the growth of a feudalistic anarchy in much of Northern France, it also marked the beginning of agricultural development and better estate management and a new money economy in trading centre and local market alike, which were to continue in certain areas during the period to come.

The Kamakura Shogunate, A.D. 1185-1334

When the great family-warrior alliance of the Minamoto clan triumphed over its Taira opponents in 1185, it resulted in the creation of a new political system to rule Japan which we call the Shōgunate and which in various forms was to last until 1868. Yoritomo, the Minamoto leader, set up his headquarters or *bakufu* at Kamakura on the edge of the Kantō plain far from the Imperial capital, and there at once began to institutionalize his rule. He did not desire to destroy either the Imperial structure or its bureaucracy at Kyōto or in the provinces, but to make his own power effective and maintain throughout Japan a security which the Imperial government and its officialdom had shown they could not provide. The warriors who led his coalition to a victory over the Taira, known as *gokenin* or honourable housemen, and who seem very similar to Carolingian *vassi* and *fideles*, pledged allegiance to him personally, though such pledges appear to have been open-ended and not contractual as were those which came to be prescribed by Carolingian proto-feudal practice. In return for such allegiance, Yoritomo gave to these warrior *gokenin* extensive grants of land, or *shiki*, often hereditary in nature, using property scattered throughout Japan which had belonged to the Minamoto family or was confiscated from his Taira foes. In return for such grants these *gokenin* were expected to serve him until death and take their regular tours of guard duty at both his own capital or *bakufu* at Kamakura or at the Imperial capital of Kyōto.

From this body of loyal magnate vassals he chose special local military governors or constables, called *shugos*, who, after 1190, were placed in almost every province in the land. They did not replace local imperially-appointed governors picked by Kyōto, but served side by side with these latter. *Shugos* were in charge of the maintenance of public order and handled the police power in their provinces and were also expected to supervise the *gokenin* whose estates were located there. Because of the danger that such *shugos* or constables might be tempted to become independent of Kamakura, Yoritomo and his successors kept the right to dismiss them at will and generally chose men for such posts who were not natives of the provinces in which they served.

In addition to *shugos* and *gokenin*, who bear a close resemblance to Carolingian counts and *vassi dominici*, still another group of less important *gokenin* warrior vassals was established throughout Japan by the Kamakura *bakufu*. These were warriors who were appointed as land stewards or *jitōs* and given authority over the estates of absentee court aristocrats, religious establishments, or those of the Imperial family which were spread throughout the land. In theory such *jitōs* had the duty of protecting the rights and income of absentee landlords of such estates, as well as maintaining local order and seeing that they were properly managed, in return for which they were allotted a share of estate income, known as a *shiki* (see page 24). In practice *jitōs* increasingly tended to take over actual control of the estates to which they were assigned as protectors, much as the noble 'protectors' of church lands did in tenth- or eleventh-century Northern France. Initially these land stewards were much more numerous in the eastern part of Japan, that old centre of Minamoto power, than they were in the western area, but their use spread rapidly in the course of the Kamakura Shōgunate, as will be noted.

To regularize this system the Emperor was persuaded, in 1192, to appoint Yoritomo as Shōgun, or generalissimo, a kind of permanent Mayor of the Palace, which implied that the latter had the duty of maintaining peace on the national level. Thus was born an office which for centuries was to exercise a power which overshadowed that of the Emperor himself. Until 1199, when he died, Yoritomo exercised power personally. Soon thereafter, however, control over the Kamakura Shōgunate passed into the hands of another family, the Hōjōs, who exercised authority as hereditary regents between 1205 and 1334, even though until 1226 puppet Shōguns continued to be chosen from the Minamoto family, and after that the office was held by a series of aristocrats and Imperial princes. These Hojo regents continued Yoritomo's system of controlling Japan by maintaining authority over the warrior class with the assistance of a council of leading *gokenin.*

In a real sense this system was a family one, for vassal *gokenin* who did Kamakura's bidding pledged not only their own loyalty but also that of their entire extended family, and this bond was an hereditary one. Orders were not only issued from Kamakura but also locally to such families by provincial *shugos*, and it was through family heads that the command to report for guard duty or to pay special levies reached those expected to obey. A well-ordered centralized government by vassalage, based upon Kamakura and reaching down through the *shugos* and local *gokenin* family heads, throughout the thirteenth century increasingly came to replace the authority of the older court aristocracy and court officials or that of the great religious establishments and estate owners of the land.

This process seems to have been accelerated when in 1221 Go-Toba, an abdicated Emperor, raised the standard of revolt in Kyōto and attempted to throw off the yoke of Kamakura. The revolt, known as the *Shōkyū* War, was suppressed and as a result several thousand estates belonging to rebellious landowners and religious establishments were confiscated and distributed to loyal *gokenin* followers, either outright, or to manage or 'protect' as land stewards. Since these estates lay mainly in the west, where warrior supporters of the Shōgunate were least numerous, this confiscation increased the authority of Kamakura over the entire country. It also led to greater power for the Shōguns in Kyōto itself.

What was perhaps an even more important result of this revolt was the issuing in 1232 of a new legal code, the *Jōei Formulary*, which fitted the needs of the warrior class and which established a legal system of importance for the entire country. The courts and laws it established not only regulated land and disputes between *gokenin*, but also came to do the same for non-feudal landowners as well. It did not do away with older Imperial law but tended in practice to be used in place of it in many cases, as well as serving as the basis of all later feudal Japanese law codes. Once formulated and applied, it gave a special organized and legally valid structure to the warrior rule of the Kamakura Shōgunate.

By the early fourteenth century, however, Kamakura's authority began to decline, just as that of the Carolingians in late ninth-century Northern France had done. One reason for this may have been a growing land hunger among the warrior class whose estates, when divided among heirs, as was the custom, became too small to support their warrior status. The problem became especially acute because by this time Japan's internal frontier in Northern Honshū no longer existed as a place where warriors could go and carve out dominions for themselves at the expense of the tribal peoples who lived there. No longer could they follow the example of Yoshitsune, after his break with Yoritomo, and go to the North, the Japanese equivalent of the American Western frontier. Such warriors now had to look for disorders closer to home from which they could profit.

Connected with this was a dissatisfaction which arose out of the results of the successful resistance to Mongol invasion attempts in 1274 and 1281, when the Japanese warrior class was successful in repelling the invaders. The warriors who accomplished this feat, *gokenin* and others as well, desired land as a reward for their efforts, and they found that Kamakura could not find enough to meet their expectations, despite some confiscation of estates which still belonged to the court aristocracy. Finally, the last Hōjō regents were young and spoiled and lacked the ability of their predecessors. As a result dissatisfaction increased, and when the able and ambitious Kyōto Emperor Go-Daigo revolted and attempted to re-establish Imperial rule in 1333, the Kamakura Shōgunate collapsed and ushered in the very different age which we call that of the Ashikagas.

In surveying the entire period when Kamakura held sway over Japan, however, it seems possible that historians have tended to overestimate the extent of its domination using heavily armed mounted warrior bowmen tied to an all pervasive vassalage system which centered in the Kamakura *bakufu*. No doubt such warriors were the élite troops of the period, as were the somewhat similar armed mounted warriors of Carolingian France. But other troops were certainly used as well. The illustrated scrolls which date from this period, for instance, show us battle scenes in which much use was made of infantry forces which must have been recruited from other segments of the population. And it is significant that the battle of Dan-no-ura, which broke the power of the Taira, was a naval battle, not one fought on land, and thus involved troops who were not mounted warriors. Indeed the traditions concerning it which are contained in the thirteenth-century *Tale of the House of Taira* specifically refer to such troops and distinguish them rather scornfully from the mounted warriors of the Kanto who were Yoritomo's trusted followers.

Furthermore, there were obviously a large number of aristocratic warriors, owning estates, who had no bonds of vassalage linking them firmly to Kamakura. Unless we assume this, we cannot explain either the Shōkyū Revolt of 1221 or account for the number of non-*gokenin* warriors who successfully defended Kyushu against the Mongols, or who were still available to support Go-Daigo in 1333. We must accept the fact then that not all of Japan's upper classes were completely organized in a network of feudal relationships, despite the *Joei Formulary*, and that instead we have here a society in which military skills and expertise were rather widely diffused among the entire population, as was the case in eighth- and ninth-century Carolingian domains.

Yet we should not concentrate our attention so exclusively upon the warrior class and its activities in Japan, that we neglect other segments of the Japanese people and their activities, for this was a period in which a great deal of progress was made in the agricultural sphere and in industry and commerce. As in Northern France much new land was being cleared and reclaimed in Japan in Kamakura times; northern Hōnshu and other mountainous regions had been settled by the end of the thirteenth century for the first time and, although her rulers did not issue any coins of their own, the growth of towns began to show how important commerce was becoming. Sakai and other ports hummed with a new commercial life, just as did Carolingian trading places, and began to communicate in a new way with Sung and Kin, China and Korea. It seems significant, as a matter of fact, that traditions relating to the battle of Dan-no-ura in the Inland Sea, already alluded to, mention a number of ships built in China which were used by the Taira forces. We also learn of temple complexes which, in addition to their religious role, began to serve as important centres for the local exchange of a variety of products of all sorts.

And if landlords and peasants were steadily putting more land into cultivation, as primitive trading places became towns and temples assumed market functions, we also find evidence of superior skills being developed by the growing artisan class. It is important to note, for instance, that Japanese swords of the twelfth and thirteenth centuries show a workmanship superior to those produced anywhere east of India or Damascus, revealing a degree of artisan sophistication not found earlier. Thus the Kamakura Shōgunate arose in Japan which, like Carolingian Northern France, had already created the basis for a better agriculture and a new merchant and artisan class in its towns, which were to be important in all later developments enjoyed by the Japanese people.

Some similarities and differences

Historians have long been aware of the similarities between the Kamakura Shōgunate and the Carolingian era as regards their proto-feudal development, and the preceding pages have emphasized this fact. It is equally important, however, to note the differences between the two. The first one, valid for almost any period in Japanese history, as a matter of fact, is the greater reliance upon families and family connections there than was the case in Carolingian France. But probably more important is the fact that the Shōguns and regents of the Mina-moto and Hōjō families who ruled from Kamakura never replaced the older Yamato family in Kyōto and became Emperors. Instead of acting like Pepin the Short, they remained hereditary Mayors of the Palace. And we must also emphasize that these Japanese Emperors remained powerful enough to provoke a Shōkyū War in 1221 and bring down the Kamakura Shōgunate itself in 1334.

Not only did the Imperial house survive with considerable power, so too did the capital of Kyōto, and elements of the civil aristocracy and bureaucracy which continued to function in the provinces side by side with the *shugos, gokenin* and *jitos* who owed fealty to Kamakura. This dual governmental system at the heart of Japanese life and in its pro-vincial centres had no counterpart in Carolingian domains after Pepin became King of the Franks. Equally interesting is the survival of a land-lord class of aristocrats whose allegiance to Kamakura was minimal, as events during the thirteenth and fourteenth centuries made very clear.

Also, when we turn to Carolingian France, we find that there, once this line had been crowned rulers of the Franks by the Popes, they came to exercise an authority within their Empire which combined that of the Emperor and Shōgun and had no Japanese counterpart either. They were not only heads of the Church in a certain spiritual sense, jointly with the Papacy, they also headed it as an institution. This explains why they not only appointed Church officials but could also hope to use them in their rudimentary bureaucracy and link them to their persons by proto-feudal bonds of loyalty quite similar to those demanded of secular counts and *vassi dominici.* Kamakura's control over Japan's religious establishments and their priests and monks was never theocratic in the Carolingian sense, nor could it consider using them regularly as officials. Its control had perforce to be limited to the appointment of land stewards on monastic temple estates—a much less direct system of keeping the religious class of Japan subservient.

On the other hand, if Kamakura failed to establish anything like Carolingian control of the religious elements in its society, its *bakufu* proved able to exercise a much more rational centralized authority over that segment of the warrior class which owed it a proto-feudal allegiance. Its *gokenin* swore a much more open-ended allegiance to its Shōguns than was found in limited, reciprocal Carolingian lord-vassal arrangements, and Kamakura elaborated in the *Jōei Formulary* a legal code binding on vassals which was much more complete than the piecemeal legislation provided by Carolingian *capitularies.* The Shōgunal authorities also kept the practice of removing *shugos* or provincial constables longer than their Carolingian counterparts, who had largely lost this right by the time of Charles the Bald's reign.

Finally, for all its weakness and incompleteness, the Kamakura Shōgunate was able to maintain internal and external peace better than Carolingian rulers were able to do. Except for one uprising we find no Japanese equivalent of the long and destructive civil wars in Francia during the reigns of Louis the Pious and his successors—civil strife that became endemic by the late ninth century when a Robertian house arose to share an elective kingship with its Carolingian rivals. And where monarchs in Northern France found themselves powerless to protect their realm from Viking pirates, Kamakura Hōjō regents were able to repulse two better organized Mongol seaborne invasion attempts. If the rule of the Kamakura Shōgunate was in some respects less complete than that of the Carolingians in Northern France, it must be admitted that it proved right up to its demise a good deal more effective.

CHAPTER IV

The First Feudal Age

Feudal Principalities in Northern France, A.D. 900-1108

By the first years of the tenth century a new age had dawned in Northern France which Marc Bloch characterized as the First Feudal Age. Today we are increasingly aware of the complexity of this period and the difficulty in finding meaningful generalizations to describe it, since recent regional studies have shown that immense differences existed between various areas of Northern France and their feudal characteristics and practices. Elements of feudalism existed everywhere, some representing decayed Carolingian forms, some new practices, but they lacked precision and definition during these years.

Perhaps it would be best to turn our attention to the king and the power he was able to exercise, and then consider the great nobles and the smaller ones as we view what was to become the more fully developed feudalism of the high Middle Ages. When we do so, we are at once struck by the steady shrinkage in the power and authority of the French monarchy. This had begun even before 900 during the reign of Charles the Bald and especially after the nobles passed over the Carolingian line to choose as their king Eudes (888-98), who represented a rival family and was descended from Robert the Strong, the powerful Marquis of Neustria. Eudes was hardly recognized at all in either Brittany or south of the Loire. And although the nobles returned to the Carolingian house in electing King Charles the Simple (898-923), this state of affairs continued. By the mid tenth century Northern French kings never visited the Midi and ceased to be recognized as monarchs there except in a perfunctory fashion. Their effective area of power and influence had shrunk until it was only found in a region between the Scheldt and the Loire, where the great nobles still did homage to the king for their *honors* but otherwise for the most part ignored him.

This process was intensified throughout the tenth century by a continuous rivalry over the kingship between the Carolingian and Capetian houses, which caused a certain alternation in those elected from each family. When Charles the Simple died in 923, Northern

French secular and ecclesiastical magnates first chose as their king Robert, the brother of Eudes, and then Robert's son-in-law, Rudolf of Burgundy. In 936 they returned to the Carolingian house and elected three kings from it in sequence—Louis IV (936-54), Lothair (954-86), and Louis V (986-87), even though the most powerful man in Northern France was Hugh the Great, Marquis of Neustria, who died in 959. Not until 987 was the issue finally settled with the election of Hugh Capet (987-96), who began a line of Capetian kings who were to rule without interruption until 1328.

The effect of this century of rivalry proved disastrous to royal power and influence. Each family had to bargain away its rights and much of its land to noble families to gain support for its royal claims—losing in the process that portion of the royal *fisc* which had survived from the ninth-century Carolingians, and much of the land and authority which had been accumulated by the Capetians in their great Marquisate of Neustria.

Nor did this end with the election of Hugh Capet. Instead it continued during his reign and those of his successors, Robert the Pious (996-1031), Henry I (1031-60), and Philip I (1060-1108). Robert, it is true, was able to gain the Duchy of Burgundy for his family, but had to establish a cadet branch there which soon removed this region from royal influence. And despite considerable effort, none of these Capetians was able to recover the Duchy of Lorraine from the German Emperors who were its overlords. Thus, by the late eleventh century, royal authority in Northern France had come to be confined to direct control over family domains in the Île-de-France (see Map I, page 16), shared with a group of smaller barons and castellans, authority over a number of abbeys and bishoprics surrounding these domains, and somewhat nebulous homage from the great lords of Northern France. For instance, when in 1071 Philip I attempted to intervene in Flanders and summoned his great secular and ecclesiastical vassals and those of his domain, he could only collect a force of twenty-seven small feudal contingents, that from Normandy numbering only ten knights in all. Obviously the military element upon which Carolingian rulers had relied in establishing their proto-feudalism had shrunk to almost nothing as far as eleventh-century Capetain kings were concerned. Except in a theoretical sense these Northern French monarchs now had no effective military power based on feudal ties which they could exercise close to their own royal domain.

One finds the same evidence of a decay of royal authority when one examines the royal court. It was a duty of a vassal to give counsel as well as aid to his lord, according to Bishop Fulbert of Chartres writing to the Duke of Aquitaine in 1020, yet increasingly during the tenth and eleventh centuries the great vassals of the French king neglected to attend the royal court. By the late eleventh century royal charters show us that the monarch was only assisted by a few loyal churchmen and a body of knights from his household and his own royal domain. Royal administration, like royal military might, now had little basis in a set of larger feudal relationships.

When one turns from the king to the great nobles, however, one finds the same situation, for disappearing royal authority was not effectively taken over by great nobles, despite their efforts to form their own principalities, feudal in nature, which worked better than that of the monarch. But before we come to any firm conclusions in this matter, we need to examine in some detail just how these great nobles operated on the local level and what these principalities were which they were attempting to make into viable alternatives to royal authority (see Map on page 16).

The origins of some of the principalities lay in the late Carolingian period. Thus Poitou was a surviving Carolingian county, Brittany a duchy containing tribal elements which had never been really incorporated into Charlemagne's Empire, and Burgundy a march which was a truncated descendant of the Burgundy of Merovingian and Carolingian times. Others developed out of great marquisates which had been established to protect Northern France from the Vikings or for other reasons. Flanders was created by two powerful nobles of the late ninth and early tenth centuries who were related to the Carolingian family, Baldwin I and Baldwin II, the royal Île-de-France was the surviving part of Robert the Strong's Marquisate of Neustria; and the County of Auvergne was what was left of the Aquitaine of Duke William the Pious. Normandy was based on lands given to the Viking chieftain Rollo in 911 by Charles the Simple and rounded out of the conquests of his immediate successors.

Further principalities began to appear somewhat later. Anjou was carved out of the Marquisate of Neustria by an able family who began as viscounts and who, by the early eleventh century, had established their authority firmly in this part of the Loire valley. The Counties of Blois and Champagne arose thanks to the marriage alliances and activities of a noble house descended from Count Hugh of Vermandois. One of Hugh's descendants, Thibaut III, late in the eleventh century, got control of a number of small counties most of which were later on made into the more consolidated County of Champagne by Thibaut IV. The Principality of Bourbon grew slowly into a relatively effective feudal state from a small castelry. Some regions such as Picardy and the lands which lay south of it and north of Champagne, or the region between the Île-de-France and Auvergne, never developed any principalities at all in this period, but remained a welter of unstable smaller ecclesiastical lordships, counties, viscounties and castelries controlled by lords of varied status and power.

It is when one examines the way in which by the late eleventh century, these embryo principalities were organized, however, that one begins to doubt the degree of their effective feudalization despite the considerable efforts of those who ruled them. A recent examination of early Norman ducal charters, for instance, makes it clear that in Normandy a considerable degree of pre-feudal Carolingian organization of its *pagi* or smaller administrative jurisdictions and officialdom survived, so that a truly feudal organization of the Duchy can hardly be ascribed to any period before the time of William the Conqueror (1035-87). The same thing is true of Flanders, where a portion near its new towns had been well organized by its counts and their castellans by the late tenth century, but where in the western region a number of subordinate counts of Boulogne, Hesdin and Saint Pol remained relatively free of comital authority until the early twelfth century. By the first decades of the eleventh century, Anjou seems to have become a well-organized feudal principality with its castles under comital control, but the nearby County of Tours, annexed by the Angevins, was much less so. Poitou kept a certain Carolingian institutional unity until the late tenth century, but then its viscounts and castellans began to become increasingly independent. Brittany, Burgundy, Champagne, and Auvergne, like the Île-de-France until the time of Louis VI (1108-37), really had no centralized feudal organization at all. Viewed as a whole then, with a few partial exceptions, one cannot really talk of an organized feudalism on a local level in Northern France during these years but rather of a varied, unstable, and anarchical system of political arrangements with various degrees of feudalization and order which held sway over the entire Northern French scene.

If one cannot speak of feudal principalities in any meaningful way during these years, there is also a need to emphasize that the same thing is true before 1108 of feudal landholding. Already in the late ninth century we have noted that many magnates had managed to transform benefices given to them into allodial property. This trend obviously continued. As a result, recent studies have shown that by the eleventh century in most of Northern France the prevailing method of holding land was allodial, and that the noble landlords of the time depended little upon feudal arrangements in the matter of their property. This seems to be especially true in Burgundy, Champagne and Auvergne, dramatically so in Picardy and Brittany, and to a considerable extent in Poitou, Normandy, Anjou and Flanders. It thus seems fair to say that a majority of the landowners, great and small, who formed the fighting aristocracy of Northern France, perhaps as many as seventy per cent of them, held their estates allodially and not by feudal ties. And even those who held property on a feudal basis did so for only a portion of their land, often from multiple lords, some less powerful than they, and thus this relationship was hardly a meaningful one.

The question which needs to be answered is why it was that, as royal power declined, the great nobles of Northern France—the counts, the dukes, and the marquises—found they were unable to form real local principalities of their own and transform Carolingian proto-feudalism and feudal relationships into an effective system dependent upon them personally. Perhaps one can best find the reason for their failure if one examines a special new military system that arose in Northern France during these disordered decades. This was the growth and proliferation everywhere of castles, and the appearance in these fortresses of a new and different class of mounted *milites* who formed the garrisons.

In Northern France castles had begun to appear in some numbers during the late ninth century in response to the threat of Viking invasions, but until the middle of the tenth century they were not so numerous that they tended seriously to compromise the efforts of the aristocracy, which had survived from Carolingian times to rule their local areas. About 950 this began to happen here, as it did in the nearby Midi, in Lorraine, and even in Italy at about the same time.

At first castles were either small, free-standing, stone towers or residences of a local magnate or landowner which were surrounded by a ditch and protected by a wooden palisade. By the late tenth century, perhaps starting in Anjou, this latter type of fortress had become the so-called motte and bailey castle in which a central mound, the motte, was thrown up within the ring-works and a residential fortress was placed upon it. Such a fortress could be easily constructed with impressed peasant labour, but was much more difficult to capture than earlier fortified structures. It spread rapidly throughout Northern France and was the type of castle which William the Conqueror introduced into England after 1066 with such success. By the late eleventh century some of these motte and bailey fortresses began to have their central keep built of stone, which rendered them even more formidable, though they were so expensive that only powerful lords with considerable revenues could afford them.

Wherever they appeared in large numbers, and they did so everywhere except where strong local princes like the Counts of Flanders and Anjou or the Dukes of Normandy forbade their construction, they limited the authority of local rulers, for the marquises, counts, and viscounts of this age who now exercised public authority seldom had sufficient dependable troops to capture them, or if they did so, could not hold them permanently. Those in charge of these new castles, then, came to enjoy a *de facto* independence, and as time went on were able to use this to ignore feudal ties and transform the land they controlled into private allodial property.

Furthermore, the *milites*, who formed the permanent garrisons of these castles, were a very different breed from the feudalized landowner *vassi* and *fideles* who had composed the Carolingian aristocracy. They were recruited from among the smaller landholders, or even represented men who had arisen from the servile class and who had now become full-time mounted warriors tied to their castellans by personal arrangements which, though feudal and representing elements that had survived from the earlier age, had little connection with the world that lay beyond the castle in which they lived. They were a new and relatively numerous class of full-time *milites*, quite different from anything known earlier in Northern France, and who did not fit very well into any larger political structure—feudal or otherwise. The assimilation of this class of *milites* into aristocratic ranks took several centuries, as we can see when we examine the story of Raoul of Cambrai, which tells of the relationship between a member of this class and his overlord in the Northern France of the late eleventh century. We note the same thing when we study the smaller seigneuries and castelries of the Île-de-France, controlled by families like the Montmorency and the de Coucy who could and did successfully defy their overlord, King Philip I.

As effective power came to be exercised on a local level by such minor barons and castellans and the *milites* who garrisoned their fortresses, a new seigneurial element in this society appeared also. Such

lords and their *milites* began to dominate the neighbouring countryside in a way quite different from that found earlier. They enforced
'protection' upon the peasants living near their fortresses in the form
of an imposition of foodstuffs and labour extorted from them, and the
charters of the period are full of complaints about these 'bad customs'
or *usages* which arose as a result. They were particularly ruthless in
their domination of neighbouring religious establishments, and their
constant feuds bore heavily upon the average peasant who found himself frequently an innocent victim of their constant turbulence. As
time went on, what emerged was a kind of castle jurisdiction which
came to be called a *mandementa*, and which often replaced the older
manorial system in parts of Northern France. Such castle *mandementas*
have been carefully studied with regard to the late tenth- and early
eleventh-century society of Poitou, of Picardy, of the Mâconnais, of
Champagne, and of Auvergne. In Auvergne they became so all-perva-
sive that they even resulted in a regrouping of the rural population,
which took up residence in new villages or *vici* near the castles themselves. A new and different serfdom thus began to be found, depending
not upon an older organization nor based upon village manors, but
upon these new castleries.

It was in precisely those regions where this new militarized castle
class was most numerous and the older authorities were least able to
deal with it, that we find an attempt to impose order by means of the
places did not disappear during this period, especially in those parts of
landlords, and peasants who found themselves at the mercy of the
turbulent castle *milites.* This was essentially a vigilante movement,
not based upon feudal ties or relationships but territorial in nature,
which attempted to proclaim a new public order after assembling the
leaders of local areas in public gatherings to enlist their aid. It began to
excommunicate lawless *milites* and castellans and take military
measures against them and even to destroy their castles. As the movement spread through Poitou, Auvergne, and other disordered parts of
Northern France, it attracted the attention of more powerful nobles,
such as the Dukes of Normandy and the Counts of Flanders, who
encouraged it in their own domains and gave it support. Its development is another proof of the general weakness of feudal ties in much of
Northern France at this time, and of the powerlessness of attempting to
use such bonds of loyalty to impose any kind of feudal order upon the
new warrior class of the period.

Nevertheless, one can already begin to see a new feudalism arising, as surviving elements of Carolingian proto-feudalism began to interact and mingle with the newer loyalties which had developed in the castle milieu of the tenth and eleventh centuries. It is true that a great church-man like Bishop Fulbert, already mentioned, tended to list the duties a vassal owed his lord in a way which still echoes Carolingian practice as described by Dhuoda, and that powerful nobles like Count Fulk the Black of Anjou or Hugh the Great could still refuse to allow the here-ditability of some of the fiefs they had given to vassals—which was an earlier Carolingian view of things. On the other hand, in Picardy during this same period, it was castle-guard arrangements, anything but Carolingian, which concerned the fighting warriors of the province. And a vassal in Burgundy in 1096, in receiving a fief from the chapter of Saint-Vincent-de-Mâcon, found it necessary to swear feudal loyalty to the latter in a formal ceremony before being able to enjoy it.

Similarly, though the legal system of Carolingian times lingered on in Poitou and Normandy—one which was still essentially territorial and non-feudal—we do find tenth-century courts in the Mâconnais beginning to be held with a personnel present whose ties were essen-tially feudal rather than territorial in nature, thus becoming feudal courts. The same thing was also happening, as noted, with royal courts in the Île-de-France by the eleventh century. And the *Song of Roland* can describe a treason trial for Ganelon as one which stressed feudal ties as the important ones. Gradually and sometimes imperceptably, a new type of feudalism had come to pervade the Northern French countryside as new bonds of loyalty were forged between the great nobles of the time and the militarized *milites* and castellans who domi-nated local areas. In most regions, however, such a development was still a tentative, inchoate, and incomplete one, and the system which was taking shape was still relatively ineffective.

It must not be supposed that this militarization of society, when a new class of *milites* and castellans arose and began to dominate the Church and the nearly peasantry, and when political fragmentation of an extreme sort became the order of the day, took place in an age lack-ing in money or in elements of economic progress. Quite the contrary. It is interesting to note, for instance, that mints did not disappear throughout this period, though they tended to be taken over by local lay and ecclesiastical lords who now issued coins in their own name and not that of their royal overlord. And coin finds dating from the tenth century show us that this money circulated widely, though on a more local basis than had been the case during Carolingian times, while a great lord like Count Gerald of Aurillac in Auvergne had sufficient money to pay his soldiers in cash rather than in land. By the eleventh century one of the great abuses in the Church against which the Gregorian reformers directed their energies in Northern France was *simony* or the sale of Church offices by the king and the aristocracy for money. Such an abuse could not have occurred had money not existed in relatively large amounts.

Furthermore, recent studies have shown that Carolingian trading places did not disappear during this period, especially in those parts of Flanders and Northern France which were affected by their proximity to a relatively prosperous Anglo-Saxon England, or to a North Sea which continued to support an active commerce. And if this was true of the tenth century, everywhere after the year 1000 a general revival of trade took place which began to increase the size of the merchant and artisan groups, who had settled in the shadow of the walls of many of the castles and monasteries which were rapidly becoming real towns. As this happened, land began to be cleared again as the peasant population increased and trade spread through the interior once more on a scale unknown since the late ninth century. By 1108 new economic currents were beginning to transform the society of the Northern France of this first feudal age into that of the high feudalism of a later era.

The Ashikaga Shōgunate and the Daimyōs, A.D. 1334-1568

The end of the Kamakura Shōgunate in 1334 ushered in a period of disorders which lasted six decades and which in many ways modified the political and social structure of Japan. The effort of the Emperor Go-Daigo (1288-1339) to overthrow the Hōjōs of Kamakura succeeded, but his attempt to set up direct Imperial rule failed. Instead, a powerful warrior leader, Takauji (1305-58), who headed the Ashikaga family, took over, and in 1336 forced the Emperor to abdicate and made the latter's successor name him Shōgun with his residence located in Kyōto. Since the Ashikaga Shōguns later on lived in the Muromachi section of the capital city, their rule is often referred to as the Muromachi Shōgunate. Takauji's success, however, proved to be only a partial one, for the deposed Go-Daigo proceeded to flee to the mountainous Yoshino area south of Kyōto and there organized a rival court and capital which lasted until 1392.

This resulted in a continuous civil war in which each court and faction competed for the loyalty of the aristocratic landowners, the civil and military officials, and the warrior class of fourteenth-century Japan, much as the Carolingian and Capetian families attempted to enlist the support of somewhat similar groups in Northern France between 888 and 987. Consequently, by 1392 two major changes had occurred in Japan. First of all, these years of disorder led to a final destruction of those older estate rights in the countryside which belonged to the absentee court aristocracy and the religious establishments, even though such rights had already been severely limited by the Kamakura Shōgunate. Now instead of the income of such estates being divided between owners and 'protectors', it tended to fall completely into the hands of local warriors who were established in these outlying provinces. The process was a slow one, but had been completed by the late fourteenth century and resulted in most court aristocrats being reduced to poverty.

Secondly, the establishment of the new Ashikaga Shōgunate almost at once resulted in an increase in the power of the *shugos* or provincial constables, so much so that they can now be referred to as *shugo daimyōs*. No longer were they assigned to districts where they had no local roots, as had often been the case in Kamakura times. Instead, the opposite tended to be true. And they were also able everywhere to make their offices hereditary and to begin to convert local shōgunal vassals into personal ones owing allegiance to them rather than the Ashikaga *bakufu*. As this happened, and they increasingly came to exercise greater authority within their local districts, they began to combine their military power with civil authority which had earlier belonged to provincial Imperial governors, who now simply disappeared. Thus these years saw the old Imperial officials cease to function at the very time that the old estates of the court aristocracy ceased to bring the latter any revenue.

Faced by this new set of circumstances, the Ashikaga Shōguns made an effort to control the growing independence of the *shugo daimyōs* by giving many of these offices to men who were representatives of cadet branches of their own family (see Map on page 20). But this policy proved relatively unsuccessful also, for by 1370 about half of the constables were from families which were not related to the Shōgunal line. Many of these latter, such as the Akamatsu, the Kono, the Takeda, the Ouchi, and the Ōtomo, were located in the heartland of Japan, surrounding the Inland Sea. In short the Ashikaga Shōguns were never able to control all of the country as the Kamakura Shōguns and Regents had done before them. Instead, by the late fourteenth century, they found themselves in a situation similar to that which came to exist in Northern France during the late ninth and early tenth centuries, when power was steadily slipping out of royal hands into those of the counts and marquises who were becoming all but supreme on the local level.

Nevertheless for a brief period after 1392 a certain equilibrium was maintained between the power of the Shōguns and their *bakufu* in Kyōto and that of the *shugo daimyōs* in the provinces. This was especially true during the reigns of the third Muromachi Shōgun, Yoshimitsu (1368-94) and his immediate successors, when special Ashikaga codes, which modified the older Kamakura *Jōei Formulary*, tended to exercise an influence over the entire warrior class of Japan. But this equilibrium proved an unsteady one indeed. So much so that after some years of relative peace in Kyōto and the provinces a new civil war broke out in 1467-77 known as the Ōnin War. The disorders which attended this struggle affected both the capital and more remote provincial regions rather dramatically. It ended in the ruin of the Emperor, the court aristocracy, and the Muromachi Shōguns alike, though the latter continued to drag out their existence for another century before they disappeared from the scene.

If the Ōnin War ended the effective power of the Ashikaga Shōguns, however, it also tended to ruin that of the provincial constables, for reasons that are rather hard to assess. It has been asserted that one cause of this was because there was a tendency for many of the *shugos* to stay in Kyōto to safeguard their interests at court, which resulted in their neglecting their own local areas and their vassal arrangements in the countryside upon which their power was based. But perhaps other factors were at work, too, such as continued disorders and an increasing emphasis upon the building of castles which in Japan, as in Northern France, caused a new military aristocracy to arise, which was hard for the *shugo daimyōs* to control.

Whatever the cause of all this, the end of effective *shugo daimyō* authority ushered in a period of even more intense disorders which lasted at least a century. These years saw the rise of this new warrior class on a local level, whom we can call *daimyōs*, just as the late tenth century in Northern France saw older Carolingian noble families lose authority in the countryside to a new class of castellans and warrior *milites*. In Japan this resulted in a feudal age which formed quite a contrast to that which had preceded it.

There are a number of differences between the way these new *daimyōs* operated from the late fifteenth century onwards and the way in which warriors had functioned in the Kamakura and early Ashikaga periods. In the first place, although some of these *daimyōs* were rooted in older constable families, most of them were new men arising on the local level with little interest in the Imperial or Shōgunal organization which continued to exist at Kyōto. They numbered perhaps several hundred in all and their domains were of varying size, some as large as a province, some as small as a castlery, and the boundaries of their lordships were shifting and unstable. In short, they bear a striking resemblance to the lordships and embryo principalities which were beginning to emerge in Northern France during the late tenth and eleventh centuries.

Secondly, although the practices they followed owed something to those found during the Kamakura era and that of the Ashikagas prior to the Ōnin War, there were certain new features about their operating procedures. For instance, the dependent warriors who served these *daimyōs* were no longer generally known as *gokenin* or housemen, but rather as house vassals (*kashin*), hereditary vassals (*fudai*), or direct vassals (*jikishin*). Some were also called *tozama* or allies, which meant warriors who had been subdued by a *daimyō*, who then entered his service, but who were not as close to him as his other vassals. These terms seem to emphasize that now personal service rather than family ties were predominant among warrior followers of a *daimyō*, in contrast to the earlier situation which had prevailed. And all vassal retainers now tended to be tied to their *daimyō* lords by formal oaths of allegiance and written oaths of loyalty which were contractual in nature and sworn before a host of dieties, thus providing us with another similarity between this *daimyō* period in Japan and the first feudal age in Northern France.

Especially important was the fact that this formal tie of sworn allegiance increasingly came to be cemented by a definite grant of land or a fief given by a *daimyō* to such retainers. This no longer consisted of a *shiki*, or fixed share in the proceeds of an estate, but of the entire estate itself. A new term also came to be used for the rights which a vassal exercised over this estate. An estate thus held was called a *chigyō*, which came close to what was meant in Northern France by feudal possession or even a *mandementa* controlled by a castelry. The income from such a *chigyō* was no longer divided, as had been the case earlier, between its ultimate proprietor and he who controlled it, like the Kamakura *jitōs* or land stewards. Instead he who was given a *chigyō* enjoyed its total income.

Finally, late Ashikaga *daimyōs* seem to have made an effort to keep the lands which they granted their vassals intact, since they supported them in wars, by encouraging the practice of primogeniture, just as had begun to be the case during the late eleventh century in Northern France. Attempts were made to forbid retainers to alienate their land, and the military service owed to a *daimyō* by these new-type vassals tended to be carefully regulated in accordance with the type and size of the estates which they held. There is ample evidence, though, that despite such attempts at regulation, ties between lord and vassal remained essentially unstable. Vassals changed lords repeatedly, and treachery seemed to be the order of the day, even though multiple homages and lordships were unknown in Japan.

Under this new *daimyō* system we note for the first time the appearance of large numbers of castles, and indeed it was probably the castle which made the *daimyō* possible. The earliest castles of the fifteenth century were rather simple affairs consisting of a central fortress surrounded by outworks or palisades and located on a hill top or near a river, which could be diverted around the fortress to form a moat. As the sixteenth century progressed, however, there was a tendency for such fortresses to become more elaborate, perhaps because of Western European influences which reached Japan through contacts with the Portuguese. Interestingly enough this development also parallels what happened in Northern France during the eleventh and twelfth centuries.

Military forces used by the *daimyōs* similarly began to change their character. Warfare became much more professional than had been the case earlier, and there was a growing tendency to use footsoldiers in battle, as well as heavily armed cavalrymen, as was the case in late eleventh century Northern France, judging from the forces mustered by William the Conqueror for his invasion of England in 1066. In sixteenth century *daimyō* Japan, however, a far more valid reason existed for an improvement in military tactics and for more elaborate castle fortifications. This was the introduction of the musket and the cannon in about 1540, which made infantry recruited from the lower classes effective against mounted warriors and which rendered obsolete the smaller, simpler castles of the late fifteenth and early sixteenth centuries.

Where *daimyō* control was particularly strong, it began to affect peasant communities profoundly as well. One way in which this happened was in bringing about a certain rationalization of peasant organization—even in some cases setting up a peasant village system with which it was easier for a *daimyō* to deal, something akin to a Northern French manorial or *mandementa* system. We know much less than we would like to about changes of this sort in the countryside during this time of troubles, but we do know that they were often rather profound in character.

Interestingly enough also, this period in Japan, like the parallel period in Northern France, saw considerable resistence to *daimyō* rule by certain segments of the population, especially in the central heartland of the country. Here two groups often found *daimyō* control especially repugnant—the great religious establishments and a segment of the peasantry, above all those living in mountainous regions. Thus monks of the great Tendai order and others near Kyōto armed themselves and as early as 1488 drove off predatory *daimyō* forces, and continued to do so for many decades thereafter. Similarly in certain provinces, as early as 1429, peasants and small landowners began to form leagues to free entire regions from *daimyō* control, movements which continued with varying degrees of success throughout much of the sixteenth century. Japan, then, during these years had its equivalent of the Peace of God movement which we find in eleventh century Northern France.

Again, as in France, this new feudalism did not arise in a period of great economic stagnation and depression. In fact, quite the contrary is true, for during the Muromachi Shōgunate, despite political weakness and fragmentation, the Japanese made considerable progress in the material sphere of their life. This was an age of great agricultural and commercial revival. One aspect of this was an almost continuous improvement in Japanese agriculture through diking, draining, and putting new rice lands and other areas into production, as well as the development of a more efficient cultivation system through the introduction of new varieties of crops.

As this happened, the commercial growth which had already begun in Kamakura times gathered force. In part, this was local in nature. Japanese technological progress, which was already considerable by the twelfth and thirteenth centuries, gathered momentum as the handicraft industries, especially weaving and metallurgy, became better organized into something like Western European craft guilds, and these began to penetrate into more remote parts of the country. So too did merchants, who banded together in organizations called *zas*, not unlike European guild merchants. Money, which had been rare until late Kamakura times, began to become more abundant. And much of it in the form of copper *cash* coinage was imported from China, so much so that already by the late fifteenth and sixteenth centuries money-lending and primitive banking had begun to appear.

As in Northern France, craftsmen and merchants began to settle in the shadow of the castles and great religious houses and transform these latter into something like towns. Other centres became even more urban, especially Sakai, which showed it was able to govern and protect itself like the twelfth or thirteenth century communes of Flanders. A merchant class with power and money grew rapidly, especially in the heartland close to the Inland Sea.

This commercial impetus spread far beyond Japan's borders as well, for now Japanese traders and pirates began to operate in increasing numbers along Chinese and Korean coasts, despite the efforts of Korean and Ming authorities to curb and control their activities. They traded arms and other products to areas of the East Asian mainland in return for silk and money, and this commerce became an important factor in the Japanese economy. The Satsuma lords of Kyūshū, for instance, began to assert control over the Ryukyus as a result and to gain for themselves an overseas island empire.

Apart from evidence of opposition to these activities in parts of Central Japan, it must not be supposed that all this took place *despite* the new *daimyō* aristocracy of late Ashikaga times. The opposite often seems to have been the case, for most of these latter, like the eleventh-century Dukes of Normandy or the Counts of Flanders, encouraged economic progress because it brought them new resources. They welcomed the settlement of merchants and groups of artisans in the shadow of their castle walls. They encouraged agricultural changes, too, by the sixteenth century, if not earlier, and helped in the draining of marshland and in exploiting mining and forests within their domains. They used these new sources of revenue to improve their own administrative machinery within their principalities, and levied taxes upon the peasantry in money rather than in kind. They thus participated vigorously in forming the new Japanese society which was to emerge by the late sixteenth and early seventeenth centuries.

We can thus divide this Ashikaga age in Japan into two rather distinct eras. The earlier one lasted until the Ōnin War, during which Ashikaga rule was imposed on most of Japan, following the long civil war between rival Imperial courts which characterized most of the fourteenth century. This was the time when a transfer of real power into the hands of *shugo daimyōs* or constables occurred, who on a local level combined the earlier authority of civil and military governors and that of the *jitōs* or house stewards and presided over the final liquidation of the *shōen* estate system which had supported an absentee court aristocracy. These constables achieved this by a network of local warrior alliances which they came to control.

Then followed, in the wake of the Ōnin War, a different century which saw the end of the last vestiges of Imperial and Ashikaga power in Kyōto and the destruction of the authority of the *shugo daimyōs* in the provinces as well. In place of both, there emerged a new age of local militarism of a different sort. In central Japan some religious establishments, some peasants, and a few towns were able to develop the power to protect themselves against disorders, but elsewhere this was an age of a new type of *daimyō* warrior living in newly arisen castles which dominated the countryside. These warriors developed a set of feudal relationships which were different in many ways from those which had prevailed earlier. Their ties were contractual, and they were allotted actual fiefs. It was also an age of vigorous economic expansion in agriculture, in foreign and domestic commerce, and in the exploitation of Japan's natural resources. The new *daimyō* class encouraged this growth because it added to their own wealth. They were thus in some ways a catalyst which helped to bring it about and which in doing so helped to lay the basis of a more prosperous Japan in later centuries.

Some similarities and differences

The parallel between the first feudal age in Northern France and the Ashikaga period in Japan seems to be a remarkably close one—even more so than that of the Kamakura and Carolingian eras which preceded each of them, respectively. As has been noted, almost every feature of Japanese feudal development duplicated what had happened in Northern France. Each period began with a long struggle between rival claimants to the central authority, great provincial magnates benefiting by it to take over entire provinces. Then both the older central and regional authorities lost their power as anarchy came to prevail everywhere and new castles arose. In these castles in each region we find a new class of feudalized lords who came to dominate local regions by using a new set of vassal followers organized somewhat differently from that which had previously been the case. Even the fact that this change came about when commercial centres were arising and a more prosperous agriculture was emerging represents a parallel between the two.

If there is a contrast, it lies in two things. In the first place, in Japan the centralized authority of the Ashikaga Shōguns and the regional power of the *sugo daimyōs* lasted much longer and were more effective than that of the late Carolingian–early Capetian monarchs and great marquisates and comital families of tenth century France — even though in the end they all suffered the same fate. Furthermore, one cannot help but be struck by the greater degree of economic and cultural sophistication which Ashikaga Japan possessed when we compare it to that of the first feudal age in Northern France. In some ways in Japan this age, from an economic and intellectual point of view, more nearly approximates that of twelfth and thirteenth century Europe than that of the eleventh century, except in limited areas such as Flanders. These differences aside, it is remarkable to find in two societies, so remote from each other and so much the product of different civilizations, an institutional and social pattern of development which seems so similar.

CHAPTER V

The Flowering of Feudalism

High Feudalism in Northern France,
A.D. 1108-1328

Between 1108 and 1328 there developed in Northern France an organization or rationalization of the inchoate, confused, and anarchical feudalistic relationships and tendencies which characterized the first feudal age into what can be called High Feudalism. When relatively complete by the late thirteenth century, a local and royal order had been imposed upon a Northern French society of largely independent lords and their *milites.* At the same time feudal practices had come to be elaborated and organized into new patterns which also affected the Church, the rising burghers of the towns, and the peasantry in the countryside. And as this feudalism, considered as a governmental system, became more elaborate, a new ideological mystique appeared, called chivalry, which also grew to be a pervasive force in this society.

The process was a double one. It took place on the local level as the great noble vassals of the king began to organize their principalities, using a more ordered set of feudal ideas, practices, and institutions. And it proceeded on the royal level as Capetian kings began to rule their royal domain more effectively and then moved out to impose a royal feudal order and administrative controls upon Northern French society as a whole.

Some of the great noble families of the time, however, began this process earlier than the Capetian house (see map on page 58). By the late eleventh century the Dukes of Normandy and the Counts of Anjou, Flanders, and Poitou had already begun to establish a more centralized feudal order in their nuclear possessions and to expand their territory. The best case in point is that of the Duke of Normandy, who not only conquered England and became its king, but also absorbed the County of Maine and exercised much influence over Brittany. Even earlier the Counts of Anjou had taken over the County of Tours and were operating south towards Poitou, just as the Counts of Flanders had expanded their rule to absorb nearby areas subject to the Emperors of Germany. And we can see the same process at

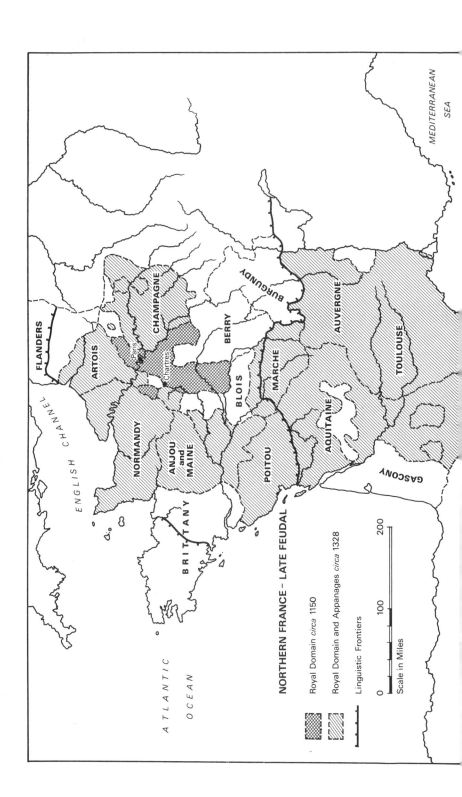

MEDITERRANEAN SEA

ENGLISH CHANNEL

FLANDERS

ARTOIS

NORMANDY

Paris

Chartres

CHAMPAGNE

ANJOU and MAINE

BLOIS

BERRY

BURGUNDY

BRITTANY

POITOU

MARCHE

AQUITAINE

AUVERGNE

GASCONY

TOULOUSE

ATLANTIC OCEAN

NORTHERN FRANCE – LATE FEUDAL

Royal Domain *circa* 1150

Royal Domain and Appanages *circa* 1328

Linguistic Frontiers

Scale in Miles

0   100   200

work as the Counts of Poitou, styling themselves Dukes of Aquitaine, entered the Limousin and in 1053 came to be recognized as overlords of Gascony.

Even less important nobles, such as the Counts of Boulogne and Brittany and a group of powerful Norman families, joined the Norman Duke in his English conquest and as a result were given important estates across the Channel in the British Isles. Nor did the process end with immediately contiguous territory, for these years saw Norman knightly families establishing themselves in what was to become the Kingdom of Two Sicilies and taking advantage of the First Crusade to become Princes of Antioch. They also saw the house of Boulogne provide Princes of Edessa and the first King of Jerusalem before 1108.

During the next two centuries this tendency intensified, if any thing, on both the Northern French scene and on the international level as well. The house of Blois-Champagne organized Champagne as a well ordered principality late in the twelfth century, controlled England and the County of Boulogne under Stephen (1137-54), produced a king of Jerusalem, and by the thirteenth century had become kings of Navarre. One branch of the Angevin house in the person of Henry II (1152-89) absorbed the lands of both the Norman dukes and the house of Poitou to form the Angevin Empire of the British Isles and continental France, while his relatives became the successful mid-twelfth-century kings of Jerusalem. The Counts of Flanders provided a line of thirteenth century Latin Emperors of Constantinople, and the Capetian house of Burgundy furnished men who became the kings of Castile and Portugal.

Even minor houses proved to be remarkably successful in this kind of enterprise, witness the Poitevin Lusignans who became kings of Jerusalem and Cyprus by the late twelfth century, the Burgundian Villhardouins who came to rule much of Frankish Greece or the De Montforts of the Île-de-France who briefly held Toulouse and then went on to make a place for themselves as great barons in thirteenth-century England.

High Feudalism, then, developed in Northern France during a period when the great vassals and the rear vassals of the Capetian kings were organizing effective feudal principalities at home and expanding their authority on the international scene. Faced by such competitors the wonder is that the Capetians were able to organize a royal feudalism and a royal authority at all during this period. This is a reality which needs to be fully grasped before we can understand High Feudalism in Northern France between 1108 and 1328.

With this in mind, let us turn our attention to the French Capetian monarchs themselves. In 1108 when Louis VI (1108-37) succeeded to the throne, he had little authority over his own domains in the Île-de-France (see map on page 58) and beyond them only a certain influence over some nearby abbeys and bishoprics, and a recognized place as overlord of most of the great Northern French nobles, though such overlordship did not yet carry with it any power to call out the effective military forces of his vassals. Louis VI managed to establish authority over the royal domain after bitter conflicts with minor barons and castellans, to keep control over the nearby Church officials, and maintain a theoretical overlordship over his great Northern French vassals by playing one side against another during the rivalries which took place among the sons of William the Conqueror, and by intervening in a disputed succession in Flanders. In 1124 he was even able to rally Northern French princes and towns in a united effort to turn back an invasion attempt by the German Emperor Henry V. With his reign, royal power and influence began to grow.

At first his son, Louis VII (1137-80), seemed well on the way to a spectacular increase in royal authority when he married Eleanor of Aquitaine and added her lands to those of his house. But by 1153 he had lost both her and her domains to Henry II of Anjou, Normandy and England. Thenceforth he and his successor Philip II (1180-1223) were on the defensive against what seemed to be the overwhelming might of the Angevins in Northern France, at least until the death of Richard Coeur de Lion in 1199. Yet Louis VII was not only able to survive this threat and use the quarrels between Henry and his sons to force the Angevins to acknowledge him as the feudal overlord of their French lands, but also to do much more. He extended his authority steadily over the French Church and over the towns of Northern France beyond his domain, gaining support from the latter by granting them charters. He was even able to secure a recognition of his position as overlord from the Count of Toulouse in the Midi.

It was Philip II, however, who infact made royal authority a reality. At first Philip had little success against the Angevins, other than making them recognize him as their feudal overlord, but after the death of Richard all this changed. Philip was not only able to secure a condemnation of John (1199-1216) from his royal French court, but also to use this as an excuse to seize John's most important

Northern French possessions—Normandy, Maine and Anjou—and add them to the royal domain. At the same time, he expanded his authority to annex Artois and Vermandois to the north and Auvergne to the south. By the time of his death in 1223, the French kings were the direct rulers of much of Northern France which was now part of their royal domain, and increasingly powerful overlords of most of the rest (see map on page 62).

What Philip II had begun was continued during the reigns of his immediate successors. His son, Louis VIII (1223-26), although he failed in an attempt to conquer England from John and Henry III (1226-72), was able to annex Poitou to the royal domain and secure a claim to Toulouse, which Simon de Montfort had seized during the Albigensian Crusade. Even more notable was the success of Louis IX (1226-70), his son. By 1259 Louis had not only forced Henry III to accept the loss of Normandy, Maine, Anjou and Poitou, but at the same time to agree that he held Gascony as a fief from the French Crown. Meanwhile, when the last Count of Toulouse died without male issue, Louis was able to annex half of his lands to the royal domain and establish his brother Alphonse of Poitiers as ruler of the rest which he held as an appanage fief. He also persuaded the King of Aragon, who had Southern French claims and possessions, to give them all up except for the town of Montpellier. At the same time he supported his brother, Charles of Anjou, in the latter's taking over the County of Provence and establishing himself as King of Two Sicilies in Italy. It was thus during Louis IX's reign that the French kings expanded their authority over most of the Midi and reached the Mediterranean.

Philip III (1270-85) and Philip IV (1285-1314) continued to expand French royal power and influence. During Philip III's reign the lands of Alphonse of Poitiers reverted to the royal domain, when the latter died childless, and under Philip IV, known as Philip the Fair, Champagne was absorbed, Montpellier encroached upon and also territory to the east nominally subject to the German Emperor. Philip the Fair, it is true, had less success in his efforts to assume direct control over Flanders and Aquitaine where Edward I of England (1272-1309) proved a worthy opponent, but he did establish the fact that both were held from the French king as feudal overlord. Thus when the Capetian family died out in 1328 and the collateral Valois branch took over, the old *Regnum Francorum* had been transformed into a real feudal *Regnum Francie*, or Kingdom of France, which

This portrayal of an attack on Dinant Castle by William the Conqueror's troops is part of the Bayeux Tapestry (c. AD 1085). It gives an early view of the motte and bailey castle which helped to create conditions in which a true feudalism could flourish. It also shows both the armament and tactics of Northern French warriors during this First Feudal Age. Though there had been changes in armament since Carolingian times, the lance was still the principal weapon. (From *The Bayeux Tapestry*, Penguin, 1949)

stretched from the English Channel to the Mediterranean and from the borders of Germany to the Atlantic.

It must be emphasized that in changing their Northern French *Regnum Francorum* of feudal overlordship, barely recognized by the great nobles, into a truly feudal French kingdom, Capetian monarchs were simply acting like other centralizing feudal princes of their day. The structure they created was a feudal monarchy, even though it may well be true that Philip the Fair and some of his ministers had begun to think and to act in ways which were more modern than that. We have several proofs of this. In the first place during the thirteenth century, at the moment of greatest royal expansion, Louis IX allowed his father's will to be carried out, and allotted to his brothers appanage fiefs such as Artois, Picardy and Anjou which were carved out of the royal domain and whose only tie with the king was one of vassalage to the Crown. He also allowed his brother Charles to hold Provence and his Italian kingdom without exacting from him any feudal ties whatsoever, because they lay in the sphere of Imperial and Papal overlordship, respectively. It was only an historical accident—not design—which saw Alphonse of Poitiers die without issue and his fiefs revert to the Crown. It did not happen with Provence or other appanage fiefs.

Similarly, the policy of giving charters to French towns, begun by Louis VII and continued by his successors, had much basis and justification in the developing feudal practices of the time. Such towns fitted into the feudal structure since they were treated as collective lordships owing military service and financial aids to the king. Their mounted sergeants were not dissimilar in the service they rendered the Crown from that demanded of noble mounted *milites.* Equally interesting is the fact that thirteenth century Capetian rulers gave a certain status or privilege to individual burgesses which marked them off from the rest of the population in a way not unlike royal vassalage.

During the reign of Louis IX even the relationship between the King and most of his great churchmen had much that was feudal about it, too, for they owed almost the same kind of service as did secular feudal lords. This is one reason why a struggle developed over their allegiance between the Papacy and Philip the Fair. Unless we consider that these two groups, the middle class and clergy, were thought of as integral parts of a royal feudal structure, we cannot understand how, when he quarrelled with Pope Boniface, Philip IV thought it natural to gather them together as separate estates on a national level

to give backing to his policies. Obviously, such estates owed their
very existence to the idea that vassals should give counsel and aid to
their lord when summoned to do so—though now this system was
institutionalized on a broader national level.

Finally we need to understand that in many ways the later Capetian
kings developed centralized administrative practices in their royal
court in Paris and in the provinces, where *baillis* and seneschals
functioned, as part of an administration which they thought of as
feudal. In this they were simply copying at a somewhat later time what
great feudal princes such as the Counts of Flanders and the Dukes of
Normandy were already doing and what the Counts of Champagne
were beginning to attempt in their efforts to perfect feudal administration. And the French kings preserved this administration when they
annexed the lands of many of these feudatories as part of their royal
domain. Witness the administration of Normandy under Saint Louis;
Anjou and Maine after they became Capetian; the way in which
Alphonse of Poitiers' centralized system was grafted on to that of the
Crown by the ministers of Philip III; or how Champagne's comital
structure became royal at the time of Philip IV. And it has again recently been emphasized that the encroachment of royal ministers
upon the rights of great French feudatories, in areas such as Flanders,
Aquitaine, or the Midi, had its justification in a *Feudal* right of appeal
from a court of a vassal to that of an overlord. One had every reason
to look on this whole development of royal power in France as essentially the growth of a more centralized and national feudalism, even
though after 1328 it was to have consequences which were to be anything but feudal in nature.

On the other hand it must be admitted that the relationship of late
thirteenth century Capetian kings to the French Church began to have
about it certain non-feudal elements which were also to be important for
the future. French monarchs throughout the twelfth and thirteenth
centuries always acted as if they were heads of their Church *in
practice,* though *in theory* they recognized supreme Papal authority
over it. Yet during the reign of Louis IX we sense a growing emphasis
upon their own sacral character as kings. Increasingly elaborate
coronation ceremonies began to stress the fact that the king differed
from his great feudal vassals in having a special religious mission or
charge, and that his control over the French Church and society in
general had a priestly element in it, as did that of Charlemagne and
Western and Eastern Roman Emperors of the time.

By the reign of Philip the Fair this tendency was far advanced, especially after he had secured the canonization of his grandfather Louis IX as Saint Louis. Thus the quarrel with Boniface VIII was more than a quarrel over the king's right to tax the clergy of France. It represented Philip's determination to assert a new kind of kingship. And when, as a result of it, the Popes had been brought to Avignon, and a great Papal order, the Templars, had been suppressed at Philip's insistence, this special religious element of the French monarchy had been made clear to everyone in France and beyond as well. A trend which was to reach its apogee much later with Bossuet and Louis XIV had appeared, and the French feudal monarchy had assumed a special religious role which was somewhat new in character.

Turning from the growth of an increasingly well organized and complex feudal order and hierarchy on a local and royal level, we need to examine another aspect of High feudalism—the way in which property was held. Here one is struck by the fact that these centuries saw a steady decrease in allodial ownership and an increase in feudal tenures. This change occurred at a rate which varied according to the regions being considered. It was noticeable earliest in better organized principalities such as Anjou and Normandy, and was slower in occuring in areas such as Brittany and Burgundy. It proceeded almost inexorably until, by the late thirteenth century, most land in Northern France was held by feudal right, and Beaumanoir, who as a lawyer was attempting to codify feudal customs in this period, could use the expression 'no land without a seigneur'. What seems to have happened was that both the kings and the great lords of the time put pressure upon the nobility to transform their lands into fiefs. They used various methods, but one of the most effective was that of finance. Thus great feudatories, like the Counts of Champagne, bought their senior vassals' allodial rights and tied them to their persons by money fiefs. Nor were French kings loath to follow their example, as a study of their money fiefs makes clear. When all else failed, then, the upper ranks of the Northern French nobility made use of money in this way to create new ties of loyalty and bring an end to independent and allodial lordships.

As land became increasingly feudalized in Northern France, we note an increase and an elaboration in feudal forms and practices themselves. Relief, which was a payment by a vassal to his lord when he took over a fief, rare earlier in organized form, became common, and so did special dues owed to a lord by his vassal, such as hospitality and the four so-called feudal aids-payments when one's lord was ransomed, went on crusade, knighted his eldest son, or married off his eldest daughter. Primogeniture became common, and the length of military service owed by a vassal was fixed by custom. Court service became a regularized duty. Ceremonies of homage and fealty became standardized and increasingly complex, and records of such ceremonies began to be written down, copying Southern French precedent in this regard. Now written and elaborate feudal codes began to appear which had the force of law in Normandy, Auvergne and other provinces. At the same time the king's court in Paris developed procedures which regulated the way in which it dealt with nobles living in its royal domain and with the great feudatories of the Crown. This was an age of elaboration and legalism which produced Beaumanoir and feudal lawyers of his ilk throughout Northern France. The *milites* and castellans who formed the lesser nobility came especially to have their land and status regularized in this way, not always to their advantage, and the greater barons found themselves tied to the king in a way which their ancestors would have considered out of the question. A new and increasingly effective feudal pyramid, legally justified, has been created in Northern France.

As this complex and better organized feudal structure emerged, it had important repercussions on the way in which Northern French aristocratic society functioned on both the local and the royal levels. This seems particularly true in the sphere of military affairs. During the first feudal age king and noble alike depended for armed service upon mounted *milites* who lived in the castles of the time and owed their overlord, whatever his rank or status, the military service of *host* (a long campaign), *chevauchée* (a raid), or castle guard, when summoned by him. Some of these *milites* lived in a separate castle, some in the household of their lord.

Now a change took place as increasingly important military contingents came to be raised by kings and great nobles from towns whose burghers owed regular military service, or from mercenaries paid in money. Indeed, it was such troops who made it possible for those who had them at their disposal to besiege castles more successfully and so end the independence of the castellan class in Northern France during the twelfth century. As time went on the mercenary element in particular gained in importance, so that a ruler like Philip II encouraged both his own great vassals and his townsmen to commute the military service they owed him into *scutage* or money payments, which he could then use to hire mercenaries who were superior to other categories of troops. This practice, incidentally, was also used by his Angevin rivals in Northern France. Thus at the very moment when *in theory* military service began to be exacted by the king and his great vassals on the widest possible basis, *in practice* the military forces used tended to be less and less feudal in character. This was true even though the king could and did still call out the entire feudal *host* as late as the first years of the fourteenth century.

Secondly, as king and great nobles became able to enforce attendance at their feudal courts as a duty owed to a lord by his vassals, one notes a tendency for such vassals to be joined at these courts by a corps of specialized administrative experts who were paid in money and did most of the work. Though many of these new feudal bureaucrats were of noble origin or soon achieved noble status, a considerable number of them were drawn from the middle class too. Thus, in effect, a feudal court class of great ecclesiastical and lay nobles found itself being replaced in power by what was becoming a corps of bureaucratic non-feudal specialists.

In the third place, money began to play an increasingly important role in the feudal system itself. It has already been stressed that great use began to be made of *scutage* in place of military service, and that loyalty had come to be insured by use of the money fief on many levels of the feudal hierarchy. But money also had even wider applications. Relief, hospitality, and feudal aids owed to a lord by his vassal came to be paid in money rather than service or kind. And so too did the fees owed by churchmen to the king and certain great lords who still in practice tended to choose them for church office. It is not surprising that by the early fourteenth century Philip the Fair could demand *aids* from local and national assemblies of estates which, being paid in money, had something about them akin to taxation—a practice incidentally which owed much to earlier Crusading levies.

Finally we note changes in the way in which the feudal noble class came to administer their own estates, whether these were secular or ecclesiastical in nature. Since money was now essential, feudal estate owners began to seek it from the lands which they controlled and discovered a bewildering number of ways to secure it. In many cases they commuted their peasants' servile status and dues to money payments and rented to these latter the land which they had previously cultivated for them. They levied new *banalités* which were dues for use of seignorial ovens and wine-presses in cash in their peasant villages and increased such dues regularly whenever possible. Some ecclesiastical estates of the period, run by the Cistercians, used hired labour and re-negotiated contracts with labourers every five years. Or kings and nobles rented out the mines and forests of their domains or the mints they controlled to entrepreneurs on a cash basis. Especially dramatic was the way certain French monarchs and great aristocratic landlords put into cultivation wastelands of forest, marsh, and fen by attracting peasants who were given land and a free tenant status in return for cash payments as they put such land into cultivation. This resulted in regular customs which regulated such land settlement and rural exploitation such as the *Customs of Lorris* or the *Laws of Bréteuil* or those which were used in the *bastides* of Alphonse of Poitiers in the Midi or of Edward I in Gascony. Even rights of justice exercised by seigneurs came to be viewed as a matter of profit in cash. The more feudalized in one sense the noble barons and gentry of Northern France came to be during this period, the more they came to behave like businessmen exploiting to the fullest the feudal and seigneurial rights which they possessed in an economy which depended increasingly upon money to function properly.

As these changes took place in the way in which Northern French feudal society actually functioned, one notes another important change taking place—the development of the set of ideals and practices which we call chivalry. This can be considered in two different ways. It represented a change in the ideas and ideals of the ruling, fighting noble and *milites* class of the tenth and eleventh century from those found in earlier *Chansons de Geste*, such as the *Song of Roland* or *Raoul of Cambrai*. Now romantic ideas of courtly love, which had their origin in the troubadour culture of the Limousin and the Midi, came to prevail, stressing romance, largesse, and courtesy as well as valour. Such ideals were in many ways essentially social in nature and not only affected those lords and ladies who eagerly followed the *Lays of Marie de France* or the narratives of Chretien de Troyes or others who wrote the popular romances of the period, but also churchmen and the Church itself. Witness the romantic cult of the Virgin and the stories told of her or even the romanticism of Saint Francis of Assisi and the Grail Legend. Whole cycles of romances were composed which dealt with Arthur and his Round Table, with Charlemagne and his paladins and with a chivalric Fall of Troy in which knight-errants fought giants and pagans, rescued damsels, or searched for the Holy Grail. These became the staple of the upper-class noble and Church society of the time and were enjoyed by other segments of the population as well. Indeed if we can believe André the Chaplain's *Art of Courtly Love*, the burghers could also welcome this courtly ideal and share in it. Nor did this chivalric society confine its interest to courtly love in the literature it enjoyed, for we know that noble audiences were equally attracted by the more earthy and cynical *fabliaux* tales of the time, such as *Renard the Fox*, which satirized the romantic tradition itself. Still other segments of this society, more pious in mood, found enjoyment in those Christian romances we know as Saints' Lives.

But if this new chivalry represented an ideal for a growing feudalized society which had its antidote in *fabliaux* realism or pious Saints' Lives, it also represented a set of practices and customs for a noble class which was beginning to attempt to institutionalize itself and set itself apart from other segments of society as the twelfth century progressed-in other words, to become a separate *order*. Chivalry was now providing a mystique and a set of practices which tended to join together the great noble feudatories and the humbler *milites* in a common social class. This order was theoretically open to all nobles, important ones and those of more modest fortune, who could join it almost as if it were a guild. The idea of a separate functional order of the nobility, of course, had precedent in earlier medieval thought. And it owed a great deal to the even earlier emergence of a separate order of the clergy which gathered strength when the Gregorian and other Church reformers had insisted upon freeing secular and monastic churchmen from feudal domination and setting them up as a special class. But now it was the nobles' turn, and chivalry provided them with their own special justification for such a separation. According to the new theory all nobles started as pages or apprentices, went up the ladder to become squires or aristocratic journeymen, and ended by becoming knights or full-fledged noble guild members after a ceremony of knighthood or a battlefield promotion, the former having strong religious connotations attached to it.

As the thirteenth century progressed there was an undeniable tendency to make this chivalric order an even more closed affair except to those whose birth gave them the proper credentials for it, and so to exclude from its ranks those who were of burgher or peasant origin. It seems probable, though, that this effort was never totally successful and that a degree of social mobility still prevailed. At the same time one must recognize that the nobility did develop its own special customs such as the tournament, hawking, and the chase, in which other groups in society did not really share. It thus came to have a social existence of its own.

We would be wise not to underestimate the power of chivalry, as it tended to set apart the nobility from the other classes of Northern French society during this period, even if they could still join it if they were able to rise in the social scale. The reason for saying this is that by the late thirteenth century social orders in Northern French society became institutionalized in the governmental structure of the time. When Philip the Fair called together his great national and local assemblies to gain support against Pope Boniface VIII, he organized them on the basis of separate estates of the clergy, the nobility, and the burghers of the towns. Thus social class stratification, which had begun as an ideal and set of practices for the nobility and clergy, became the basis of the institutions of government which prevailed in Northern France, and was to remain so until the time of the French Revolution.

Some have argued, and in a sense rightly so, that many of the developments which have been included here as aspects of High Feudalism, whether they be governmental, social, ideological, military, financial, or judicial, along with the rise of a new powerful middle class and a freer peasantry, were actually movements *away* from feudalism towards a different sort of world. They have seen in the growth of a money economy and of a paid bureaucracy and army the beginnings of the modern state, and in the new chivalry the first traces of that ideal of the gentleman which flowered during the Renaissance. One can, of course, read history in this way.

On the other hand, we need to remember that during these centuries all of this took place within a social structure which was increasingly being feudalized in Northern France, and which gave all the above developments a feudal content and form important to their very existence, and which were still being elaborated during the first decades of the fourteenth century. If the Northern France of Philip the Fair seems to possess social, economic, governmental and military features that are already modern in some ways, it was also the culmination of that first feudal age which began to take form as the Carolingian system decayed and a new feudal society took on substance during the twelfth and thirteenth centuries.

Centralization and the Tokugawa Shōgunate,
A.D. 1568-1868

In 1568 a warrior leader of the lesser *daimyō* class, Oda Nobunaga (1534-82), capped a swift eight-year rise to power by seizing military control of Kyōto and beginning the consolidation of all Japan under centralized rule. His rise had been a rapid one from the time of his defeat of the powerful *daimyō* Imagawa Yoshitomo in 1560 and his construction of a new centralized domain centred at Gifu between Kyōto and the Kantō plain. By 1573 he had deposed the last Ashikaga shogun, Yoshiaki, and ended the Muromachi Shōgunate, and had begun a series of campaigns in Central Honshū which broke the power of both the *daimyōs* and great independent religious houses of this region. Nobunaga's efforts, which by the mid-seventeenth century had resulted in a new centralized feudal Japan when they were carried on by his able successors Hideyoshi (1536-98), Ieyasu (1542-1616), and the latter's Tokugawa heirs, were not a unique phenomenon. For it is important to note that they took place when on a local level a somewhat similar feudal consolidation was taking place, as was also the case in Capetian France. This consolidation was the work of certain *daimyō* houses which by 1573 had already begun to impose a degree of feudal order in the areas which they had come to dominate. They were thirteen in number, the Ryūzōji, the Ōtōmo, the Shimazu, the Mori, and the Chōsokabe in south-western Japan and the Yamana, the Asakura, the Oda, the Tokugawa, the Takeda, the Hōjō, the Asai and the Uesugi in north-central Honshu (see map on page 72). Some of these *daimyō* families which headed regional warrior alliances were new ones. Some, on the other hand, were the descendents of older families of *shugo daimyōs* who had long held power in the regions they dominated. In this category were the Shimazu, the Ōtōmo, the Yamana, the Takeda, and the Uesugi. They thus much resemble the great feudal magnates who were powerful in late eleventh- and twelfth-century Northern France, some of whom were also from new houses, some descendents of older Carolingian counts and marquises. And it is interesting that Japanese *daimyōs* tended to be weakest in the old heartland of Imperial Japan near Kyōto and around the Inland Sea or in the lightly settled, less fertile lands of Northern Honshū. It was in this heartland that Nobunaga and Hideyoshi rose to power and consolidated their authority during the late sixteenth century and then, like the French monarchy under the late Capetians, reached out beyond to establish their authority over more distant princely *daimyōs* on the periphery.

Nobunaga's victories and success in Japan's central heartland gave him a special advantage by enabling him to keep the great *daimyō* houses of the west and the east separate from one another and thus to defeat them in detail. He also made great use of the firearms and cannon

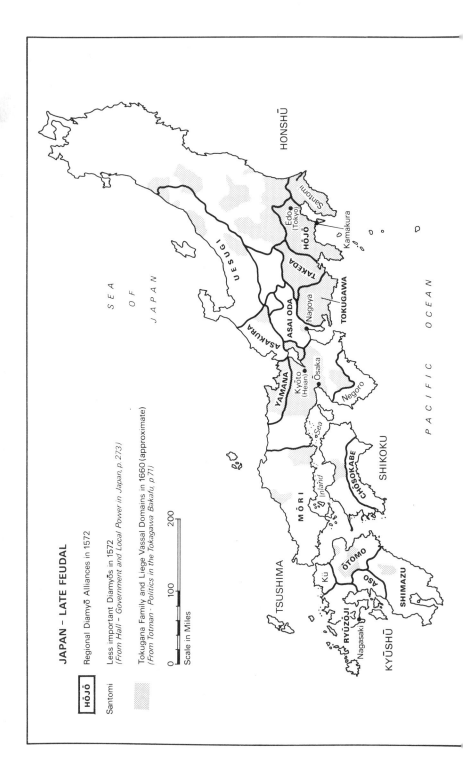

JAPAN – LATE FEUDAL

HŌJŌ   Regional Daimyō Alliances in 1572

Santomi Less important Daimyōs in 1572
(From Hall – Government and Local Power in Japan, p. 273)

Tokugana Family and Liege Vassal Domains in 1660 (approximate)
(From Totman – Politics in the Tokugawa Bakufu, p. 71)

Scale in Miles

0   100   200

HONSHŪ

UESUGI

SEA
OF
JAPAN

Santomi

Edo
(Tokyo)

HŌJŌ

Kamakura

TAKEDA

ASAI ODA

Nagoya

TOKUGAWA

ASAKURA

YAMANA

Kyōto
(Heian)

Ōsaka

Negoro

PACIFIC   OCEAN

MŌRI

Inland
Sea

CHŌSOKABE

SHIKOKU

TSUSHIMA

ŌTOMO

Kū

ASO

RYŪZŌJI

SHIMAZU

Nagasaki

KYŪSHŪ

which had been newly introduced into Japan and which made his forces superior to those of his foes. And he was an astute enough politician to win the support of each defeated rival by giving him good terms before he took on another. Thus he was well on his way to domination of all of Japan when he was murdered by one of his vassals in 1582.

His place was quickly filled by his able peasant-born general Hideyoshi who took up where he left off. By 1590 the latter, with Tokugawa's help, had defeated the Hōjō *daimyōs* who controlled the Kanto plain and was lord of all Japan. Hideyoshi, like Nobunaga, owed his success both to his superior generalship and to the way he conciliated the *daimyōs* he defeated and fitted them into his warrior alliance system. Once his conquests had been completed, he began, on a national level, to introduce certain reforms, such as new land surveys, a formal distinction between classes, and a new nationwide coinage system. He also attempted to regularize his own status by getting the Emperor to appoint him as Regent. But he was perhaps too interested in foreign adventures to concentrate his full attention upon the Japanese domestic scene, and undertook futile efforts to conquer Korea in 1592 and 1597. Thus final consolidation had to await the time of his successors, Ieyasu and the Tokugawa shōguns.

Ieyasu, who had been Hideyoshi's principal lieutenant and who had benefited from his conquests by immensely increasing the size of his family's domains, when Hideyoshi died in 1598, at once stepped into his shoes, in the process disposing of the latter's young heir. In 1603 he secured for himself the title of Shōgun, which neither Nobunaga or Hideyoshi had been able to achieve, and thus legitimized his rule in a special and traditional way. Then he and his able heirs, Hidetada (1579-1632) and Iemitsu (1604-51), despite serious revolts which took place in 1615 and 1637-38, firmly established their Shōgunate at Edo (modern Tōkyō) and gave Japan a centralized feudal rule which was to last until 1868.

It is interesting to note that Ieyasu and his immediate successors rejected the Ashikaga practice of residing in Kyōto and copied Kamakura by setting up their centre of power or *bakufu* in the more remote Edo, in the Kantō plain. This was one basis of their power, a delegation of authority from the Emperor to keep the peace throughout Japan. During the following centuries they came to elaborate this authority in accordance with Confucian principles — much as late Capetian kings from the time of St Louis onwards elaborated on the idea of the king as the special protector of the entire realm.

Their second basis of authority was their position as head of a hierarchy of feudal retainers and vassals—a feudal organization which was national in scope and which again resembles the regularized royal feudalism which was developed in France by late Capetian monarchs. And in each case there was an earlier precedent for this—in Japan the Kamakura and Ashikaga Shōgunates, in Northern France the Carolingian system of vassalage and government.

In the third place, although the Tokugawas were careful to preserve the illusion of Imperial authority and to maintain the Imperial house at Kyōto with ceremonial functions and a religious role which centred there and at shrines like Ise, they did not neglect to set up their own rival to it. They established temples at Nikko and elsewhere which were dedicated to the spirit of Ieyasu, thus giving their family a special place in traditional Japanese religious practices, just as the later Capetians did when Philip the Fair secured the canonization of Louis IX, emphasizing a royal religious role which competed with that of the Papacy. Indeed the parallel between the way in which the Tokugawas dealt with the Imperial house and the Capetians with an Avignon Papacy seems a particularly striking one.

More important than all of this, however, were the methods used by the Tokugawas to develop and organize the *daimyō* system which they had used to bring them to power. Their efforts in this direction took some two generations before they had been completed, and the system they ended up with was in many ways quite different from that with which they had started. Let us examine it in some detail.

First, by 1651 the Tokugawa *bakufu* had come to divide Japan into three categories of territory, after a ruthless crushing of the power of their potential *daimyō* rivals and a good deal of shifting of *daimyō* families from one part of Japan to another. The first category of territory was composed of lands which the Tokugawas either ruled directly or allotted to a number of smaller *daimyōs*, called *fudai*, who were devoted to their interests (see map on page 72), This territory included a large part of the richest rice lands, most of the towns, and those regions where at an earlier time most important religious sects had operated almost independently. It also included the major part of the important mining areas and controlled the natural trade gateways which made possible a monopoly of exports and imports. At strategic spots within these lands they built great castles, like those of Nagoya or Edo itself, which gave them control over internal communication routes within Japan. Perhaps we should regard all this as the Tokugawa version of the French royal domain.

Closely linked with this first category of territory was a good deal of land given to cadet branches of their house which they established in other regions that were especially important to them—an old system in Japan, as has been noted, but also one which seems similar to the Capetian establishment of appanage fiefs (see page 58). Thirdly they allowed less dependable *tozuma daimyōs* who were their potential rivals to occupy lands which mainly lay on the periphery of Japan's heartland, especially to the south-west. Even these great houses, however, and some others as well, were tied to the Tokugawas by a network of marriage alliances and the establishment of a special link to the Shōgunal house through the granting of the honorary surname of Matsudaira.

As an integral part of controlling this hierarchy of vassals, who were the warrior aristocracy of Japan, they also devised an intricate system of requiring the assistance of their *daimyōs* in the building of their great castles—a kind of feudal aid which fell especially heavily upon those vassals who lived nearby. And they required a regular attendance of their *daimyōs* and the latter's families at the Shōgun's court at Edo. Such a system went back to the time of Nobunaga and Hideyoshi but was regularized and elaborated by early Tokugawa Shōguns. It was not unlike a system found also in thirteenth-century France by which the Capetians encouraged their great vassals and their families to attend the royal court regularly.

In Tokugawa Japan *in theory* a different situation existed between those lands ruled directly by the Shōgunal house and those under the control of their great *daimyō* feudatories, just as in late thirteenth century France there was a difference between territory which formed part of the royal domain and that belonging to the great vassals of the king. Each *daimyō* was the supreme lord in his own lands with his own officials and rights of justice separate from those of the Shōgun. But in practice in Japan, as in Northern France, the central authority increasingly encroached upon such jurisdictions. In France this encroachment took the form of encouraging appeals from feudal courts to the royal courts of Paris. In Japan somewhat different methods were used. There, as early as 1615, the *bakufu* directed that in *all* matters the example of Edo was to be followed in every province. Later on, officials began to be sent out to audit *daimyō* accounts and to inventory their military resources and establish a census of the population within their domains. Actual administration of these domains remained in *daimyō* hands, but supervision was firmly in the control of the

Shōgunate. And when a number of feudal law codes, which were national in scope, had been promulgated for all of Japan by the Tokugawas, a degree of centralization had been achieved which would have been the envy of Philip the Fair, not to mention Edward I of England.

As this process of centralization progressed and internal peace continued to be maintained, a further change began to become apparent —the bureaucratization of the feudal warrior class to which the Tokugawas assigned all governing functions on a local and national level—which transformed them into a class or order of civilian officials. One way in which this process came about was through a change in the way the central *bakufu* and local *daimyōs* alike rewarded the aristocratic followers who served them. They began to change these rewards from land tenures to salaries—a kind of money fief. So general was this change that it has been estimated that by early eighteenth century ninety per cent of the warrior of *samurai* class received this kind of emolument. The forms of feudal loyalty between lord and vassal on a local and national level were preserved, but in practice a new kind of aristocratic civil servant had been created who differed considerably from his turbulent sixteenth-century predecessor. And since these years saw an increasing use of money throughout Japan and a steady inflation in prices, this made the bureaucratized *samurai* a class who were at the mercy of those authorities at Edo and on the local level who provided them with their stipends.

During this same time another change took place which represented the completion of earlier trends—the transformation of the warrior class of aristocrats and other groups of the society into distinct and different social orders. This began to happen, as we have noted, in thirteenth-century France, too, but in Japan it was much more complete and regularized. Let us see how it came about.

In Japan, this process reached its culmination when the early Tokugawas proclaimed in their law codes that there were three distinct classes in their realm: a warrior class of aristocrats, a middle class of merchants and artisans, and a peasant class of cultivators. Each of these classes or orders of society was to remain quite distinct from the others, and movement from one class to another was forbidden by law. Furthermore only the warrior class had the right to govern or to bear arms. In other words the Japanese equivalent of the Northern French division of society into orders of nobles, clergy, and middle class was established in a way which was much more complete and exclusive.

The reasons why this structured society developed in Tokugawa Japan are not easy to understand, for as late as the sixteenth century no such clear system of class distinction existed. During the earlier age great religious houses had maintained armed forces, townsmen had fought as warriors and maintained their own local governments, and even peasants had served *daimyōs* as footsoldiers or united to form vigilante bands which fought *daimyō* anarchy in whole provinces. It was thus possible for Japan to have evolved a system not unlike that found in Northern France during the high Middle Age– one where classes were not completely distinct from one another and where each could maintain military forces of its own and have certain governing functions.

That this did not happen may perhaps have been due to the way in which Nobunaga and Hideyoshi rose to power. They did so in the heartland of Japan, which was the very region where non-feudal military forces possessed by townsmen, great religious establishments, and peasants were most formidable. Thus, when these warlords crushed local opposition here, they made sure that these groups were disarmed as a menace to their authority, especially Hideyoshi, who organized what have come to be known as sword-hunts to deprive all non-*samurai* groups of their weapons. Ieyasu, who came from a more remote part of Japan near the Kantō where warrior traditions were strong, religious establishments weak, and merchant towns few in number, had every incentive to continue Hideyoshi's policies, especially since he and his successors kept direct control over this same Japanese heartland where disarmed non-warrior elements of the population were most numerous. Thus by the late seventeenth century the early Tokugawas had managed to exclude in hereditary fashion all classes except the warrior artistocracy from the practice and profession of arms or any direct role in government. What had begun as a temporary expedient had become a national policy which had important results for the future of Japanese society as a whole.

As the High Feudalism of the Tokugawas became a pervasive organized system which affected every segment of society, we also find that a set of ideas, ideals and practices arose quite similar to the chivalry of the high Middle Ages in Northern France. In part this represented a set of practices accepted by the warrior aristocracy, now increasingly bureaucratized, and which were enshrined in the provisions of the Tokugawa codes which governed so many aspects of their lives. In part it was reflected in certain popular ideals or codes of conduct for this *samurai* aristocracy which could be summed up in what was known as *bushido*, which were strongly influenced by Zen Buddhism and which seem as elaborate and studied as those which were concerned with the code of knighthood in thirteenth-century France.

Such practices were naturally reflected in the culture of the period, and can perhaps be seen most clearly when we look at Japanese drama during the Tokugawa era, which seems to have developed very much as chivalric literature did in Northern France. Drama in Japan had an ancient origin, and as early as the twelfth century had developed a tradition of Nō plays which the Tokugawas made the special prerogative of their *samurai* class. It is not this sort of traditional drama which need concern us here.

What was new was a vital theatre, popular in character, which we know as Kabuki. This appeared in Kyōto, Ōaska, and Edo in the course of the seventeenth century and was connected with both the Nō tradition and popular puppet drama. It was this kind of drama which came to embody many of the Japanese ideas as to how their upper classes should behave. At its most popular, Kabuki drama dealt with stories concerning its historic warrior past in two great cycles of plays. One of these dealt with events taking place in late Heian and early Kamakura times, the other with the sixteenth-century age of Nobunaga, Hideyoshi, and Ieyasu. Each set of plays expressed and elaborated the ideals of the warrior class with certain romantic elements added to these stories. In short this kind of drama developed in a way quite similar to that found in the romances of twelfth- and thirteenth-century Northern France which depicted Arthur, Charlemagne, and Troy in romantic guise. But there was a third source of Kabuki drama which was more contemporary in the way in which it depicted the Japanese warrior upper class. I refer to plays which dealt with intrigues at the court of the Shōguns or told of tragic events like the life story of the Forty-seven Ronin. These gave the audience, many of whom were non-noble, a sense of participation in upper-class aristocratic affairs. And finally Kabuki included in its drama an element which tended to deal realistically with other social groups, a Japanese equivalent of *fabliaux* tales. By the eighteenth century, when Edo began to attract a growing class of wealthy merchants as well as noble families, the best Kabuki theatre had its headquarters there and remained as a vital force until the end of the Shōgunate and and even later. So in Japan, as in Northern France, we find a set of ideas, ideals and conduct reflected in an artistic tradition which tended to celebrate the aristocratic class who were its leaders and other ideas were to remain important for several centuries.

If one emphasizes, as one must, the feudal nature of Tokugawa Japan as one examines its institutions and its culture, it is still possible to see here, as in Northern France, elements of a new order of things which were growing below its ordered feudal hierarchy and which were to burst into new and vigorous life when she left her feudal past behind and entered the more modern world in 1868. By the eighteenth century, for instance, as we have noted, her warrior *samurai* class had in fact already been transformed into a civil aristocracy of bureaucrats who in many ways seem to foreshadow the later Japanese civil service.

Even more important, though, is an understanding of the fact that her merchant and artisan class, though excluded from office or military service grew in wealth and power as rapidly as did their Northern French burgher counterparts of the thirteenth century. The wealthy merchant princes of Kyōto, Ōsaka, and finally Edo were extremely powerful in ways which foreshadow the *Zaibatsu* of post-Meiji Japan. Increasingly they came to control the impoverished *samurai* to whom they loaned money and even the great *daimyos* who managed the Shōgunate itself. It was no accident that it was they who were important in supporting Kabuki drama during the seventeenth and eighteenth centuries and who formed much of the audience who read the popular literature of the day. It was they too, along with the *samurai* class, who kept in touch with the scientific and other ideas of the outside world filtering into Japan throughout late Tokugawa times, despite official efforts to control this flow. And they were joined by an artisan class whose skills developed steadily and who were aware of foreign accomplishments in the technical field which reached them via the Dutch and others. So that when the *Meiji Restoration* came in 1868, noble official, merchant, and artisan alike were ready to take advantage of the opportunities offered them to help build a new Japan.

One final word is needed, however, to help us understand Tokugawa Japan, and this concerns the attitude it developed towards the outside world. And here again we find a contrast between this period and the one which immediately preceded it. During the last years of the fifteenth century and the entire sixteenth century, Japanese society seemed ready to expand its horizons in rather dramatic fashion. The Satsuma *daimyōs* of Kyūshū had come to dominate the Ryukyus to the south of them, and as early as 1480 were making sure that their kings sent tribute to the Ashikaga Shōguns in Kyōto as part of a general expansion of trade and pirates along the coasts of China and Korea. Japanese ships began to venture as far south as Formosa and the Philippines and to link the Kantō region by sea with older established ports such as Nagasaki, Ōsaka, and Kōbe. Perhaps Hideyoshi's attempts to take Korea were a part of this process. And as all this happened, European influences began to reach Japan itself directly through the Portuguese, who seem to have introduced superior firearms and new principles of castle construction to Japan. Both of these latter profoundly modified Japanese warfare, as has been pointed out. And along with these contacts came Christianity, which during the sixteenth century made many converts in Japan and especially in Kyūshū.

Yet soon after the Tokugawas had taken over, they reversed this trend, stopped outside contacts and began a policy of isolation which kept the Japanese in and foreigners out except through a few carefully controlled trade portals. At the same time Christianity was at first forbidden and then suppressed by Shōgunal authorities.

No doubt this policy was in part the result of a quite justified fear of European domination and represented an attempt to copy the way the nearby Chinese kept Western foreigners at arm's length. But it had other causes as well of a more domestic nature. Those areas of Japan in which foreign influences were more pervasive were just those regions in the south-west where less dependable *tozuma daimyōs* were the strongest. Keeping out foreign religious and economic influences, therefore, tended to curb the power of potential rivals the Tokugawas had every reason to distrust. In like manner Philip the Fair and his immediate successors in Capetian France attempted to take over Flanders and Aquitaine, unsuccessfully it is true, because both had strong links with foreign English monarchs which made them a threat to their centralized feudal monarchy. Also foreign trade in Tokugawa times benefited the very merchant class in the growing towns which the Shōguns had disarmed and which they were attempting to make subservient by the establishment of direct control over them. And the suppression of a native Japanese Christianity fitted into their policy of an increasing control over all religious establishments in the land, even to the extent of a confiscation of part of their landed wealth. The fact that Christianity had come to be strongest in Kyūshū made it doubly suspect. Thus in a special way the Tokugawa policy of isolating Japan from the outside world formed a

1 Tapestry from the Loire Valley, *c.* AD 1500, called 'The Triumph of Youth' and depicting the chivalric ideal of Western Europe. It shows that this tradition continued to be powerful in the more modern age which reached Northern France by 1500. (From W. Wixom, *Treasures of Medieval France*, Cleveland Museum of Art, Ohio, 1967)

2 This rare illustration of a helmeted Merovingian warrior, *c.* AD 600, from an engraved belt buckle, shows the armour which such warriors wore. They do not appear to have been very different from the late Roman soldiers who preceded them. Obviously the essential change to mounted warriors using the stirrup had not taken place in any decisive way in Merovingian Gaul at this point. (From J. Hubert, J. Porcher and W. Volbach, *Europe in the Dark Ages,* Thames & Hudson, 1969)

3 A lacquer statue of a helmeted Japanese guardian god from Nara, *c.* AD 742. It shows what a Japanese warrior of this period at the Imperial Court must have looked like. The armament is generally similar to that current in Merovingian France, and it seems obvious that the stirruped warrior had not yet appeared in the Japan of this era. (From S. Warner, *Japanese Sculpture of the Tempyo Period*, Harvard University Press, Cambridge, Mass., 1964)

ET SYRIAM SOBAL· ET CONVERTIT
IOAB· ET PERCUSSIT EDOM INVAL
LE SALINARVM ·XII MILIA·

4 Mounted Carolingian warriors, late 9th century (illustrated in *The Golden Psalter of St Gall*). These warriors, using the lance and stirrup, had become the élite soldiers of the era in Northern France and an important factor in Carolingian proto-feudalism. The illustration gives an accurate idea of their armament and equipment and shows, interestingly, that except for fighting on horseback, they appear similar in armament to the Merovingian warrior in Plate 2. (From J. Broussard, *The Civilization of Charlemagne*, trans. by F. Partridge, McGraw-Hill, 1968)

5 Mounted Japanese warriors, mid 13th century (from the scroll entitled *The Burning of Sanjo Palace*). This illustration, dealing with events in the mid eleventh century, was actually drawn some two centuries later. It depicts Japanese warriors of Kamakura times who made much use of the bow, in contrast to the lance, the chief weapon in the Carolingian West. (From *Collected Japanese Scroll Paintings*, Vol. IX, Kadogowa, Tokyo, 1964, in Japanese)

6 Castle of Crac-des-Chevaliers, Syria, 12th and 13th centuries. The best-preserved Crusader castle, it resembled similar castles in Northern France which have disappeared or are in ruins. The walls are of stone and intricate outworks surround the central keep. Such a castle was almost impregnable, except after a long and arduous siege. (From J. LaMonte, *The World of the Middle Ages*, Appleton-Century-Crofts, 1949)

7 Nagoya Castle of Ieyasu's time, early 17th century (destroyed in the last war). It shows the different way in which the Japanese constructed castles during the 16th and 17th centuries when a centralized feudalism took over and was completed by the early Tokugawa Shōguns. Guns and cannon were by then in common use in Japan and they demanded a different type of castle construction from that used in Northern France during the period of centralizing Capetian Feudalism. (From L. Warner, *The Enduring Art of Japan*, Harvard University Press, Cambridge, Mass., 1965)

8 Illustration of a scene from a Kabuki play, late 17th century, showing how the society of Tokugawa Japan enjoyed such a spectacle. Kabuki emphasized both the martial past of Japan, shown by the two central actors in this plate, and also singing and dancing, and so resembled the chivalric tradition of Western Europe. (From Haruo Suwa, *A Garland of Kabuki,* Kadogowa, Tokyo, 1970, in Japanese)

conscious part of their system of centralized feudalism, which might have been less successful without it.

The flowering of Japanese feudalism under the Tokugawas, then, which completed the work of Nobunaga, Hideyoshi, and other more local daimyōs, managed to create by the mid seventeenth century what was probably history's most ordered and complete feudalism, although it was certainly by no means a static system as some have claimed. It turned Japan over to a class of feudal warriors who ruled it and organized it in a military fashion. Its centralized feudalism, controlled by the Edo *bakufu,* organized each class of society into an order legally quite separate from the others, while at the same time maintaining control over Japanese religious establishments. It helped create its own chivalric ethos in the literature and drama it patronized. It was to last until the middle of the nineteenth century and to it we owe much that still remains distinctive in the Japanese spirit and in Japanese society.

Some similarities and differences

Again one cannot help but be impressed by the similarities between aspects of High Feudalism in Northern France and the feudalism which developed in Japan after 1568, a fact which the previous pages have emphasized. Such similarities are not just in the way feudal institutions and practices developed but also in the institutions themselves. Yet differences are equally important. Three seem espeically decisive. During these years in Japan the Imperial house survived along with its theoretical and symbolic authority, even though the Shōgunate developed newer kinds of influence which competed with it much more than had been the case in earlier times. At the same time that strong family element in Japanese feudalism, which was rarer in Northern France, was actually strengthened by the Tokugawas after they had completed their organization of Japan. And in the third place Tokugawa feudalism was much better organized and more complete than the system which the Capetians were able to develop by 1328.

Important as these differences are, there are two others which deserve emphasis as well. First of all no Capetian ruler ever desired or came close to achieving anything like the isolation from the outside world which the Tokugawas and their feudal bureaucracy managed to impose upon their state. Despite a captive Papacy at Avignon and a measure of control over its subjects, late Capetian kings always thought of France as part of Western European Christendom and did not desire to withdraw from it. Such was obviously not the case with Japan, which after 1603 not only closed its doors to Europeans, but to its East Asian neighbours as well, although the isolation it achieved was never a total one.

Secondly, the Northern French aristocracy never achieved that monopoly of office and the profession of arms which characterized the feudal warrior class in Tokugawa Japan. Despite the growth of distinct orders in its society, such groups remained anything but functional in practice. The middle class in Northern France was never disarmed, as Courtrai proved to Philip the Fair's great sorrow, and it was the mercenary soldier without class allegiance rather than the feudal aristocracy who often dominated the battlefield. On the governmental side burghers served as royal administrators and kept control over their own town governments, which did not happen in Japan. We also continue to find in Northern France a use of the clergy in administration which had no Japanese parallel whatsoever. The directing forces of High Feudalism in Northern France thus had a broader basis than did those of the Tokugawa Shōgunate, and this in many ways made the transition to a more modern state easier to achieve. Even Northern France's peasantry were never completely kept from rising in the social scale and joining the governing classes, as was the case in Japan after 1568.

One must thus conclude that the peculiarities one finds in late Japanese feudalism when one compares it with High Feudalism in Northern France were relatively important, and that these peculiarities make it difficult to equate these two societies except in a rather tentative fashion.

CHAPTER VI

The Feudal Aftermath

Northern France, A.D. 1328-1789

The High Feudalism of the Capetian Monarchy did not long endure after 1328. It was destroyed when the Hundred Years War showed that this system could not protect the French realm. It died on the fields of Crécy and Poitiers as the flower of French chivalry fell before the long-bows of the armies of Edward III and the Black Prince, even though the lesson these battles taught had to be repeated in the next century at Agincourt before it really sank in. It is no accident, therefore, that the royal reigns of Charles V and Louis XI, which followed these disasters, show us kings who seem to be freer of the feudal goals and ideals which had animated even the most advanced later Capetian monarchs.

Despite all this, elements of High Feudalism continued to exist in Northern France until the time of the French Revolution, even though Francis I, Henry IV, Richelieu, and Louis XIV tried hard to complete the work of Charles V. It was with some justification that the members of the French National Assembly could believe that it was they who had finally done away with the surviving vestiges of feudalism in France in 1789, an end that was enshrined in the provisions of the Code Napoléon.

To understand, however, the ways in which feudalism lasted on throughout four and a half more centuries, we need to consider a number of aspects of French society. First we should note that its centralized royal government kept many features which can be considered to be a feudalized hangover from its past. One of these was a tendency of its privileged nobility to monopolize certain civil and military royal offices and to continue to hold high Church positions. This persisted despite the humble advisors of Louis XI or the middle-class bureaucrats who served Richelieu and Louis XIV as intendants. By and large until the French Revolution, they also dominated the royal officer corps. They and the higher clergy, who were recruited almost exclusively from noble families, were also able to gain for themselves an immunity from taxation which was not extended to the middle class or the peasants. This kind of privilege was certainly a heritage from High Feudalism. So were the Estates-Generals, the Parlements, and the local estates which continued to function, in some cases throughout the eighteenth century.

Even more noticeable in early modern France was a continuation of aspects of High Feudalism on the local level. The great nobles of the period of the Hundred Years War organized private armies and continued a system of patronage which has been called bastard feudalism and which was quite similar to earlier lord–vassal relationships. Nor did this all disappear with Louis XI, for during the sixteenth century we find great nobles such as the Constable of Bourbon or the Dukes of Guise able to control entire regions of France using very much the same system. Indeed the coming of Calvinism to France and the adherence of much of the aristocracy to its cause seems to have recreated elements of the older feudal order on a local level, even though the lordship of an Antoine de Bourbon was quite different in the many ways from that exercised earlier by a John the Fearless of Burgundy or a Gaston de Foix. One may well be exact in describing the Fronde of 1648 as the last great feudal revolt in French history.

Equally striking is the continuation of feudal and seigneurial tenures and property rights, generally commuted into money payments, until to the time of the French Revolution. It has been argued that during the seventeenth and eighteenth centuries those who could claim such tenures and rights among the French upper classes, and who saw in them a chance for profit, actual extended them. They thus helped to cause a reaction and a zeal for reform that finds its echoes in the *Cahiers* of those elected to the Estates-General of 1789. It is also certainly true that feudalism as a concept was largely invented by lawyers and others during this period, who were trying to explain such property rights in an age which was increasingly being affected by the ideas of the Enlightenment. We cannot, then, underestimate the feudal aftermath as it affected property any more than we can forget how it continued as we view the nobility or royal government. It was only very gradually that Northern French society abandoned its ideas and practices and prepared itself for a post-feudal nineteenth- and twentieth-century world.

Japan since 1868

At first glance the history of the Japan which emerged with the passing of its feudal order soon after 1868 seems very different from that of Northern France between 1328 and 1789, even though the revolt of the Choshu and Satsuma *daimyō* clans which overthrew the Tokugawa Shōgunate was also very much the result of the failure of a feudal system to defend the realm against foreign incursion. In Japan's case this was that encroachment by Westerners which followed on the heels of Commodore Perry's forcible opening of Japan's gates to the outside world. As it became apparent that their feudal governmental structure could not defend them, the Japanese overthrew it and began to transform both it and their society in a way which amazed Westerners who little understood the dynamism they could muster.

After a few futile revolts the *daimyōs* and the *samurai* class were pensioned off, and a new army was organized on a modern Western European basis which replaced the Shōgunate's obsolete feudal military structure and whose members were recruited from the entire population. The civil service was thrown open to all without class distinction, and thus the entire fabric of an hereditary *samurai* officialdom disappeared. Education, already widespread, now became universal as the government assumed the responsibility of preparing all Japanese for any career for which they had the talent, and class distinctions were legally abolished. A new constitution, modelled in some ways along the lines of that of Imperial Germany, was promulgated, and a modern administrative government began to function. And much else changed as well. The older, traditional Japan of the Tokugawa Shōguns seemed a thing of the past as the Imperial house was asserted to be supreme in Japan.

It would be wise, however, to temper one's conviction that all of feudal Japan disappeared with the Meiji Restoration and its immediate aftermath. It is true that the Japanese embraced the modern state and its apparatus with a verve and a rapidity which would have caused Frenchmen of the sixteenth, seventeenth, and eighteenth centuries to regard their own progress in this direction as so halting that it was almost retrograde. Yet once this new Japan had been formed, one begins to note some special ways in which a feudal aftermath soon appeared.

These became particularly noticeable when, after 1894, Japan began to expand beyond her borders, fight wars with China and Russia, and occupy the island chain of the Pescadores, as well as Formosa, Korea and Port Arthur. This return to a policy which had been abandoned since the days of Hideyoshi caused most Japanese to stress in their modern nationalism their martial feudal past. No wonder they

encouraged *bushido* virtues among the members of their new officer
corps which echoed a *samurai* past, and that they looked to their
chivalric literature and drama for models to be emulated by twentieth-
century Japanese.

After Japan's brief experiment with a more liberal parliamentary
government between 1922 and 1930, this trend became even more
marked. As patriotic societies became more active and liberal
Prime Ministers were assassinated by those who had strong links with
the armed services and with the Kwangtung army in particular,
Japanese expansion was resumed into Manchuria and Northern China
and then beyond. To further such aims, elements within the armed
services began to take over power and form a twentieth-century
Shōgunate which pushed the Emperor back into seclusion. This clique
ran Japan until its defeat in 1945.

It was no accident that during its fifteen-year sway feudal virtues
were extolled and the warrior past of Japan was emphasized in song and
story and in the classrooms of the nation. Kabuki drama which stressed
aristocratic warlike tales was immensely popular, and Hideyoshi's
great castle near Kyoto was reconstructed in bad taste. Japan seemed
to be returning to aspects of its feudal past it had abandoned in 1868.

A second defeat in war ended this trend in 1945, and the Japanese
again plunged wholeheartedly into the more modern world with results
which still amaze us. Her professors, her students, and her youth in
general seem to have turned against the feudal past which so attracted
her recent warlords. Whether this will last, however, remains a secret
of the future which will unroll for her in the decades ahead. But one
can be certain that the wise and moderate Yoritomo, the impetuous
Yoshitsune, the brutal and pleasure-loving Hideyoshi, and the clever
Ieyasu will not be forgotten by Japan, for the feudalism they helped to
foster is still part of the Japanese heritage.

Select Bibliography

Comparative Studies

Coulborn, Rushton (ed.), *Feudalism in history*, Oxford University Press; Princeton University Press, 1956.

des Longrais, F.J., *L'est et l'ouest: institutions du Japon et de l'ouest comparés*, Paris; Tokyo, 1958.

French feudalism—general

Beeler, J.H., *Warfare in feudal Europe, 730-1200*, Cornell University Press, 1971.

Bloch, Marc, *Feudal society*, Routledge; University of Chicago Press, 1961.

Boutruche, R., *Seigneurie et feodalité*, 2 vols., Paris, 1959-70.

Duby, Georges, 'La noblesse dans la France médiévale', *Revue historique*, CCXXVI, 1961.

Rural economy and country life in the medieval west, Edward Arnold; University of South Carolina Press, 1968.

Ganshof, François, *Feudalism*, trs. Philip Grierson, 2nd edn, Harper, 1961; 3rd edn, Longman, 1964.

Genicot, Léopold, 'La noblesse au moyen-âge dans l'ancienne "Francie"' *Annales: Economies—Societies—Civilisations*, XVII, 1962.

Lot, F., and Fawtier, R., *Histoire des institutions françaises au moyen-âge*, 3 vols., 1957-62.

Strayer, J., 'The development of feudal institutions', *Twelfth-century Europe and the foundations of modern society*, University of Wisconsin Press, 1961.

Feudalism, Van Nostrand, 1965.

White, Lynn, *Medieval technology and social change*, Oxford University Press, 1962.

Japanese feudalism—general

Asakawa, Kan'ichi, *The Documents of Iriki*, Tokyo, 1955.

Land and Society in modern Japan, Tokyo, 1965.

Duus, Peter, *Feudalism in Japan*, Knopf, 1969.

Gonthier, André, 'Le régime féodale au Japon', in *Société Jean Bodin, Receuils I*, Les Liens de vassalité et les immunités, 2nd edn, Brussels, 1958.

Hall, John W., 'Feudalism in Japan: a reassessment', in *Comparative*

Studies in History and Society, V. 1962.

Government and local power in Japan, 500-1700, Princeton University Press, 1966.

Matsuoka, Hisato, 'Special features of Japanese feudalism', in *Int. Congress of Historical Sciences*, Moscow, 1970.

Robinson, Basil, *Arts of the Japanese Sword*, 2nd edn, Faber, 1970.

Sansom, George, *History of Japan*, 3 vols., Cresset Press, 1959-64; Stanford University Press, 1958-63.

Northern France—the Frankish Period

Bachrach, Bernard S., *Merovingian military organization, 481-751*, Holt, Rinehart & Winston, 1972.

Bondurand, Édouard, *L'éducation carolingienne: le manuel de Dhuoda*, Paris, 1887.

Boussard, Jacques, *The civilization of Charlemagne*, trs. Frances Partridge, Weidenfeld; McGraw-Hill, 1968.

Dhondt, Jan, *Étude sur la naissance des principautés territoriales en France*, Bruges, 1948.

Ganshof, François, 'L'origine des rapports féodo-vassiliques', in *I problemi della civilta carolingia*, Spoleto, 1954.

'Les liens de vassalité dans la monarchie franque', in *Société Jean Bodin, Receuils I: Les liens de vassalité et les immunités*, 2nd edn, Brussels, 1958.

Frankish institutions under Charlemagne, trs. B. and M. Lyon, Brown University Press, 1968.

Odegaard, Charles, 'Carolingian oaths of fidelity', in *Speculum*, VI, 1941.

Vassi and Fideles in the Carolingian Empire, Oxford University Press; Harvard University Press, 1945.

Stephenson, Carl, 'The origin and significance of feudalism', in *Amer. Hist. Review*, XLVI, 1941.

Japan—Nara through Kamakura

Asakawa, Kan'ichi, 'Some aspects of Japanese feudal institutions', in *Trans. of the Asiatic Society of Japan*, 1st series, XLVI, 1918.

'The life of a monastic Shô in medieval Japan', in *Annual Report of the American Hist. Assn.*, I, 1919.

'The founding of the Shôgunate by Minamoto Yoritomo' in *Seminarium Kondakovianum*, VI, 1933.

Gontier, Andre, 'Le Shô japonais', in *Société Jean Bodin, Receuils, III, La tenure*, Brussels, 1938.

'L'organisation générale du "Shô" japonais' in *Société Jean Bodin, Receuils IV, Le domaine*, Weteren, 1949.

Hall, John C., *Japanese feudal laws: the magisterial code of the Hōjō power-holders (1232)* in *Trans. of the Asiatic Society of Japan,* 2nd series, XXXIV, 1906.

Joüon des Longrais, F., *Age de Kamakura: sources (1180-1333),* Paris and Tokyo, 1958.

Lewis, Archibald, 'The Midi, Buwayid Iraq and Japan: some aspects of comparative feudalisms, 936-1050', in *Comparative Studies in Society and History,* XI, 1969.

McCullough, Helen, trs. 'A Tale of Mutsu', in *Harvard Journal of Asiatic Studies,* XXV, 1964-5.

Morris, Ivan, *The world of the Shining Prince,* Oxford University Press; Knopf, 1964.

Sadler, Arthur, trs., 'Heike Monogatari', in *Trans. of the Asiatic Society of Japan,* XLVI-XLIX, 1918-21.

Sansom, George, 'Early Japanese law and administration', in *Trans. of the Asiatic Society of Japan,* 2nd series, IX-XI, 1932-4.

Shinoda, Minoru, *The founding of the Kamakura Shōgunate, 1180-1185,* Oxford University Press; Columbia University Press, 1960.

Northern France—early and high feudalism

de Beaumanoir, Philippe, *Coutumes de Beauvaisis,* ed. Salmon, Paris, 1899-1900.

Dhondt, Jan, 'Les "solidarités médiévales": le Flandre en 1127-1128', in *Annales: Economies—Sociétés—Civilisations,* XII, 1957.

Douglas, David, *William the Conqueror,* Eyre & Spottiswoode; University of California Press, 1964.

The Norman Achievement, 1050-1100, Eyre & Spottiswoode, 1969.

Duby, Georges, *La société au XIe et XIIe siècles dans la region mâconnaise,* Paris, 1953.

'Les origines de la chévalérie' in *Ordinamenti militarii in occidente nell 'alto medioevo ',* Spoleto, 1968.

Fawtier, Robert, *The Capetian kings of France, 987-1328,* trs. L. Butler and R. J. Adam, Macmillan, 1960.

Fazy, Max, *Les origines du Bourbonnais,* 2 vols., Moulins, 1924.

Fossier, Robert, *La terre et les hommes en Picardie jusqu'à la fin du XIIIe siècles,* Paris, 1968.

Fournier, Gabriel, 'La seigneurie en Basse-Auvergne au XIe et XIIe siècles', in *Mélanges Louis Halphen,* Paris, 1951.

Le peuplement en Basse Auvergne durant le haut moyen-âge, Paris, 1962.

Ganshof, François, 'Les relations féodo-vassaliques aux temps post-Carolingiennes', in *I problemi d'ell Europa post-Carolingia,* Spoleto, 1955.

Garaud, Marcel, 'La construction des châteaux et les destinées de la *vicaria* et du *vicarius* Carolingiens en Poitou' in *Revue hist. de droit français et étranger*, XXXI, 1953.

Les chatelains de Poitou et l'avenement du régime féodale, XIe et XIIe siècles, Poitiers, 1964.

Guenée, Bernard, *L'occident au XIVe et XVe siècles: les états*, Paris, 1971.

Halphen, Louis, *Le comté d'Anjou au XIe siècle*, Paris, 1910.

Latouche, Robert, *Histoire du comté du Maine pendant le Xe et XIe siècles*, Paris, 1905.

Le Marignier, Jean-François, *Recherches sur l'hommage en marche et sur les frontières féodales*, Paris, 1945.

'Le dislocation du pagus', in *Mélanges Louis Halphen*, Paris, 1951.

'Les fidèles du roi de France (936-987)' in *Receuils Clovis Brunel*, II, Paris, 1955.

Le gouvernement royal aux premiers temps capétiens (987-1108), Paris, 1965.

'Political and monastic structures in France at the end of the tenth and beginning of the eleventh century', in *Lordship and Community in medieval Europe : selected readings*, F.L. Cheyette (ed.), Holt, 1968.

Lewis, Archibald, 'Seigneurial administration in twelfth-century Montpellier', in *Speculum*, XXII, 1947.

'Count Gerald of Aurillac and feudalism in south central France in the early tenth century', in *Traditio*, XX, 1964.

The development of southern French and Catalan society, 718-1050, University of Texas Press, 1965.

'The Guillems of Montpellier', in *Viator*, II, 1971.

Loomis, Roger, *The Development of Arthurian Romance*, Hutchinson, 1963.

Luchaire, Achille, *Social France in the age of Philip Augustus*, New York, 1912.

Lyon, Bryce, *From fief to indenture: the transition from feudal to non-feudal contract in Western Europe*, Oxford University Press, Harvard University Press, 1957.

Painter, Sidney, *French Chivalry*, Oxford University Press; Johns Hopkins University Press, 1940.

Pegues, Franklin, *The lawyers of the last Capetians*, Princeton University Press, 1962.

Perrin, Charles, *La seigneurie rurale en France et en Allemagne du début du IXe à la fin due XIIIe siécle*, Paris, 1953.

Perroy, Edouard, 'Social mobility among the French noblesse', in *Past and Present*, XX, 1962.

Petit-Dutaillis, Charles, *The Feudal monarchy in France and England from the 10th to the 13th century*, Kegan Paul, 1936.

Richard, Jean, *Les ducs de Bourgogne et la formation du duché*, Paris, 1954.

Strayer, Joseph, *The administration of Normandy under St Louis*, Cambridge, Mass., 1930.

'Two levels of feudalism' in *Life and thought in the early Middle Ages*, R. S. Hoyt (ed.), University of Minnesota Press, 1967.

Les gens du justice du Languedoc sous Philippe le Bel, Toulouse, 1970.

Verriest, Leo, *Noblesse, chévalerie, linages*, Brussels, 1959.

Witt, Ronald, 'The landlord and the economic revival of the Middle Ages in Northern Europe', in *Amer. Hist. Review*, LXXVI, 1971.

Wood, Charles T., *The French Apanages and the Capetian monarchy, 1224-1328*, Oxford University Press; Harvard University Press, 1966.

'Regnum Francie: A problem in Capetian administrative usage', in *Traditio*, XXIII, 1967.

The Quest for Eternity, Anchor Books, 1971.

Japan — the Ashikaga and Tokugawa periods

Bellah, Robert N., *Tokugawa religion*, Free Press, 1957.

Bowers, Faubion, *Japanese Theatre*, Hermitage, 1952; Peter Owen,1954.

Crawcour, Edward, 'Changes in Japanese commerce in the Tokugawa period', in *Journal of Asian Studies*, XXII, 1963.

Dore, Ronald, *Education in Tokugawa Japan*, University of California Press, 1965.

Hall, John C., 'Japanese feudal laws: the Ashikaga Code' in *Trans. of the Asiatic Society of Japan*, 1st series, XXXVI, 1908.

'Japanese feudal laws III: the Tokugawa legislation' in *Trans. of the Asiatic Society of Japan*, 1st series, XXXVIII and XLI, 1911, 1913.

Hall, John W., 'The castle town and Japan's modern urbanization', in *Far Eastern Quarterly*, XV, 1955.

'Foundations of the modern Japanese Daimyō', in *Journal of Asian Studies*, XX, 1961.

and Jansen, M. B. (eds), *Studies in the institutional history of early modern Japan*, Princeton University Press, 1968.

Henderson, Dan F., *Conciliation and Japanese Law, Tokugawa and Modern*, University of Washington Press, 1965.

Ishii, Ryōsuke, 'On Japanese possession of real property: a study of the Chigyō in the Middle Ages', in *Japan Annual of Law and Politics*, I, 1952.

McCullough, Helen, trs., *Taiheiki, a chronicle of medieval Japan*, Oxford University Press; Columbia University Press, 1959.

Sakai, Robert, 'The Ryuku Islands as a fief of Satsuma' in *The Chinese World Order*, J. K. Fairbank (ed.), Oxford University Press; Harvard University Press, 1968.

Sheldon, Charles D., *The rise of the merchant class in Tokugawa Japan*,

1600-1868 Augustin, 1958.

Suzuki, D. T., *Zen Buddhism*, Ann Arbor, 1958.

Tsukahira, Toshio, *Feudal control in Tokugawa Japan*, Harvard University Press, 1966.

Totman, Conrad, *Politics in the Tokugawa Bakufu, 1600-1843*, Harvard University Press, 1967; Oxford University Press, 1968.

Varley, Paul, *The Ōnin War: history of its origins and background*, Columbia University Press, 1967.

France — Valois to French Revolution

Ford, Franklin L., *Robe and Sword: the regrouping of the French aristocracy after Louis XIV*, Oxford University Press; Harvard University Press, 1953.

Lewis, P. S., *Later Medieval France: the polity*, Macmillan, 1968.

Lough, John, *An introduction to seventeenth-century France*, Longman, 1954.

McFarlane, Kenneth, 'Bastard feudalism', in *Bulletin of the Institute for Historical Research*, XX, 1945.

Major, J. Russell, *Representative institutions in Renaissance France, 1421-1559*, University of Wisconsin Press, 1960.

'Popular initiative in Renaissance France' in *Aspects of the Renaissance*, A. R. Lewis (ed.), University of Texas Press, 1967.

Perroy, Edouard, 'Feudalism or Principalities in fifteenth-century France', in *Bulletin of the Institute for Historical Research*, XX, 1945.

The Hundred Years War, trs. W. B. Wells, Eyre & Spottiswoode, 1951.

Soule, Claude, *Les états généraux de la France (1302-1789)*, Heule, 1968.

Strayer, Joseph, *On the medieval origins of the modern state*, Princeton University Press, 1970.

Japan since 1868

Butow, Robert, *Tojo and the coming of the war*, Oxford University Press; Princeton University Press, 1961.

Craig, Albert, *Chōshū in the Meiji Restoration*, Oxford University Press; Harvard University Press, 1961.

Earl, David, *Emperor and nation in Japan: political thinking of the Tokugawa period*, University of Washington Press, 1964.

Minear, Richard H., *Japanese tradition and Western Law*, Harvard University Press, 1970.

Victors' justice: the Tokyo war crimes trial, Princeton University Press, 1971.

Reischauer, Edwin O., *Japan: the story of a nation*, Duckworth; Knopf, 1970.

INDEX

Agincourt, battle of, 83

Agriculture, progress of, 32, 37

Aids paid in money, 67

Ainu peoples, 14-15, 23

Akamatsu family, 49

Albigensian Crusade, 61

Allodial property, 31, 44, 45, 65

Alphonse of Poitiers, 61, 63 64, 68

André the Chaplain, 69

Angevins, the, 13, 43, 59, 60, 67

Anjou, 42, 43, 61, 63, 64: allodial property, 49; castles, 44; Counts of, 45, 57; feudal tenures, 65

Antioch, Dukes of, 59

Antoine de Bourbon, 84

Antrustiones, 18

Appanage fiefs, 63, 75

Aquitaine, 12, 28, 42, 61, 64, 80: Dukes of, 59

Armed retainers, 18-19, 21

Art of Courtly Love (André the Chaplain), 69

Arthur and the Round Table, 68, 78

Artois, 61, 63

Asai family, 71

Asakura family, 71

Ashikaga Shōgunate, 36, 48-55, 73, 74, 80: civil war, 48-9; inability to control whole country, 49-50; codes, 50; Ōnin War, 50, 51, 54, 55;

agricultural revival, 53; commercial growth, 53-4; money and coinage, 54; increase of towns, 54; comparisons with Northern France, 55-6; end of Shōgunate, 71

Auvergne, 42-4, 48, 61: movement against castles, 46; feudal codes, 66

Avignon, the Popes at, 65, 74, 81

Baillis, 64

Bakufu (capital), 33, 34, 36, 39, 49, 50, 73-6, 81

Baldwin I and Baldwin II of Flanders, 42

Banalités, 67-8

Beaumanoir, 65, 66

Belisarius, 19

Beneficium (benefices), 19, 21, 26, 31: hereditability, 31; received from more than one lord, 31; transformed into allodial property, 31, 44

Bishops, power of, 16-17

Bloch, Marc, 10, 40

Blois-Champagne, house of, 59

Boniface VIII, Pope, 63, 65, 70

Boulogne, Counts of, 43, 59: land in British Isles, 59

Bourbon: Principality of, 43: Constable of, 84

Boutruche, R., 10

Brittany, 28, 40, 42-4, 57, 59: feudal tenures, 65